MEMOS

from

MOSES

Kevin Don Levellie

Contact Information: Kevin Don Levellie
                       17475 E 390th Road, Paris Il 61944
                       217-463-8770 or 217-712-1287
                       KDLevellie@gmail.com
                       On Facebook as Kevin Levellie

ISBN: **978-1-365-97299-7**

Also Available by Kevin Don Levellie at www.lulu.com (some titles are on Amazon):
- ❖ Contributors
- ❖ The Principles Of Existence Genesis 1-3
- ❖ Sparks From The Psalms
- ❖ Ascents
- ❖ FAQ The Book Of Habakkuk The Prophet Who Prayed
- ❖ The Pointed Jesus
- ❖ Jesus Annotated
- ❖ JESUS Blessings
- ❖ Striking Events Critical Times Triumphant People
- ❖ From Connection to Reckoning Romans 1-4
- ❖ From Out to Everything Romans 5-8
- ❖ Sailing The Three Cs Romans 9-11
- ❖ From Personal To Personnel Romans 12-16
- ❖ Comments On The Book Of Revelation
- ❖ The Learning Tree
- ❖ SAINTS not sinners
- ❖ Who Says Life Doesn't Have A Guarantee?
- ❖ Fellowship
- ❖ Ground Work memorizing entire books of the Bible
- ❖ Worship: A Primer
- ❖ Common Worship Theory
- ❖ The Gospel According To The Sons Of God A Memoir
- ❖ What Makes It Southern Southern Gospel Music
- ❖ You Have To Love It   The Value Of Classical Music
- ❖ What Does Bach Prove?
- ❖ Films: A Christian Critique And Assessment
- ❖ The Christmas Greeting Poems Of Kevin Don Levellie
- ❖ The Christmas Season
- ❖ Hickory Hog And The Christmas Rascal
- ❖ Hickory Hog Holiday Tales Volume 2
- ❖ Hickory Hog Holiday Tales Volume 3
- ❖ Hickory Hog Holiday Tales Volume 4
- ❖ The Search For Hickory Hog
- ❖ Hickory Hog Lives
- ❖ The Book Of Opinions And Observations

These entries originated as my journal entries at the Saturday morning men's journaling group in Terre Haute, Indiana.

Deuteronomy 6:4
7 March 2015

I am going to dig as deeply as I can here in the time I have, although I do not claim that I will plumb all the depths of this verse which I regard as one of the ten Old Testament Foundation Scriptures which I preached on a few years ago. Those are: Genesis 1; Genesis 3; Genesis 15; Exodus 20; Leviticus 19:18; Deuteronomy 6:4-5; Psalm 23; Isaiah 53; Jeremiah 31; Habakkuk 2:4. Obviously, it's all profitable for teaching, etc., but these are the ones that so much is built on. Genesis 1 and 3 are also covered in my book, <u>Principles of Existence</u>. I won't cover any of the ten commandments here, but they have been largely covered in many other places. We'll be looking at a lot of verses that haven't had the press that section has had.

We're used to plurals. How many things are really onlies in your life, and what would be **the** only one?

A popular song in the early 70s declared that one is the loneliest number. It was the kind of song that would appeal to a college student without a girlfriend and something which he could wallow in to almost justify his loneliness. I'm going to take the first l and the first e out and get at the real truth. One is the onliest number. I thought I had invented onliest, but I find that it is a non-standard variable of only which is what is meant. Our God is exclusive both to Himself and for us. Instead of being lonely, we have real fellowship with Him. Hear's how we know. (That's' not a typo.)

Hear. Deliberately take this in. It's the same as the opening of the 5:1 retelling of the ten commandments. This is not to be background noise.

Whatever we hear we are responsible for. It will be on the test. Since this is a command, they could refuse to hear if they wanted to, and they could flunk the test.

He said they should listen and do in verse 3. Here he tells them why.

They are **ISRAEL**. They are those who have struggled with God and overcome. We haven't overcome God, but everything else by coming to grips with God. People who reject God say they're fighting Him, but they're really not. They don't believe He exists, so they discount Him from the get go. At best they are shadowboxing, and no one ever knocked out a shadow. I don't believe Steven Hawking, for all his anti-God celebrity, ever seriously wrestled with God.

God wants wrestlers. Those who wrestle with God will wrestle for God. He doesn't want resignation – I give up – or weak acceptance – oh, all right. He wants a nation armed to their teeth with their relationship with Him.

By wrestling with God we learn His moves. We learn His strengths. We learn His power. We learn His objectives. We make contact. We can then fight the world which is so much wimpier than God.

Hearers are to be active, not passive. That's why there are so many calls to hear in both testaments.

The Lord is the Yahweh. There's only one, but He is still particularized by the article, not as though He was one out of many.

They should know Him and His name by now, even though they are the new generation. Their folks should have told them. Moses is going to leave them, so he tells them. It's not an insult to tell them something they may know when it's this. It would be an insult not to tell them. When we don't speak of God or Jesus we are insulting others. (WHOA! Do we ever do that?) We wouldn't ever say, "You're not good enough to know this," but when we don't say anything at all, it's as if we said that.

The being one is our God. Elohim (the Hebrew word for God) is the source of creation. The Old Testament makes this equivalency over and over. Yahweh = Elohim. You can't substitute on either side. Yahweh will never be less or other than Elohim. No one else besides Yahweh will ever be Elohim. It's a closed circle – Absolutely.

Oh, but we need to make room – people say. Make room for whom?

People try to do it, even Christian people. Over twenty years ago I once heard a "Christian" campus minister (not from our Brotherhood) rejoice because there was no a Muslim presence in the religious mix of the school. What folly to act as though someone could take a place beside our God! He is exclusive and allows for no pluralism.

#1. There **is** no one else. Never has been.

#2. There is no **place** for anyone else. They wouldn't fit. They can't even be made to fit like the round peg put into the square which reshapes itself as a circle in the psychological examination in the 60s television series "The Prisoner". The world will make everything fit or look like it fits. Everything except God, that is.

#3. No person will ever fit or pass the test of being Elohim.

Yahweh is **our** Elohim. Moses includes Himself. Everyone is on the same level in this regard. No one is above anyone else. No one has a better God than your God. He can beat up any other god.

Joshua later challenged the people to commit, but Moses just says flat out: Yahweh is our Elohim. It's not like deciding what team to be a fan of. There is no pluralism in the spiritual realm. You can't like two teams at the same time. There is only Yahweh. All others are pretenders or fictions.

The Lord is one. They knew of the plurality of gods on the market from the years the nation was in Egypt. Even the generation born in the wilderness who hadn't seen the images, would have probably heard the names, and been exposed to the idea of the culture of pluralism, even if they hadn't been inundated by it. I wonder if Moses was taken to the equivalent of Ra's "church" as a child?

The New Testament also subscribes to the unity. The Father and I are one. That's the bedrock of it all. No one can explain what we've labeled as the "Trinity", but it's there. You can dispense with the word if you want to, but not with Father, Son and Holy Spirit as distinct titles. The oneness doctrine held to by some Pentecostal groups does not do justice to the scriptures. Nothing more or less than Father, Son and Holy Spirit as three distinct designations will do. Without them, you almost have to throw out the gospel of John, for one thing, as well as many other passages in the epistles where there three are all mentioned in the same verse.

The world is fractured, but our God is one. Paul wrote against church fracturing in I Corinthians. If only we would go back to scripture alone, but even those whose motto is "Sola Scriptura" often have their own schematics overlaying the scriptures.

We cannot have **anything** but Yahweh in our system. Even a human outline around the scripture is wrong. I know I used one in my book on Revelation, but I only used it as a handle, not as if it were scripture in itself. I would not impose it on anyone.

One is the smallest number you can have and still be a number. Fractions don't count. They are parts of numbers. We need a whole number. One is the fewest that few can get to be. There are no dissensions or divisions in one. There is complete congruence mathematically and agreement logically in one.

One is functional. There are no divided actions or thoughts in one. God is never conflicted. Again, Jesus proclaimed that as recorded in the gospel of John. This is not the foundation of Judaism alone, but of the church as well. I wonder why it's not quoted more in the New Testament? I could only find one time, and that was in Jesus' words in Mark 12:32. Jesus doesn't go beyond it, but it could be that it was so well known among the people that there was no need to supplement or defend or proclaim it. It's kind of like we don't go around telling people that that's air they're breathing.

This is the foundation. There can only be one. More than one and the building will totter and be unstable with the variances between the different foundations.

God calls us to unite because He is unity.

No shifting shadow.

No concealed motives or agenda.

No uncertainty.

No wondering about right and wrong.

Everything about our lives – cosmology, soteriology, morality, ethics, education, everyday living, economics – is founded on the oneness of the Creator/Redeemer. There is no multiverse or alternate universes or histories. Back To The Future or the button taking you back in Galaxy Quest are fun, but no one can go back. God knows that. He doesn't even go back Himself, although I believe He could if He wanted to. He has made the present universe on the basis of a linear existence. That is a part of our make up. Eternity could well be different, but there's no way we could adequately explain it to someone else in the present space/time world, even if we understood it in our spirit. Instead of going back and redoing it with a new Adam or telling Adam enough to keep him from sin, God accepts the situation of the fall and makes provision for remedy. He redeems and restores, but He doesn't let it happen again to see if they'll get it right this time. Only a One God could do that!

Another advantage to a One God is that there are not varying requirements for varying locations or groups. I passed through a small town where at the west end there was a gas station charging $2.18 a gallon. At the east end of town, not much more than a mile away on the very same street as the first station, there was one charging $2.54 a gallon. The disparity between the two stations was even more awful because they were both stations of the same brand of gas! Some people will say that in their church you have to do everything that the Bible says plus other things, either in order to be saved or in order to be members of the church. God doesn't say that. He doesn't allow a single difference in a single congregation. He doesn't make some people do more than others to receive His grace. It's the same for all. It doesn't cost a person anymore to come into Jesus Christ in Illinois where I live now than it did in Oregon where I grew up.

One makes it easy to get it right. In a Peanuts strip or show they once showed Charlie Brown going to his closet to pick out his outfit for the day. He opened it up and all that was in there was a row of the same shirts with the zigzags on them. It was a joke, and yet it pointed out the fact of how easy it would be if there was only one, and it was right choice. Whichever shirt Good Old Charlie Brown would have picked out would have been right because we would have always recognized him in it, and since we love him, it would draw him to our attention. When we wear Jesus, we have all of God's attention.

We can trust God because He is one. He will never change or fail. He will never abandon us. That is foundation for all life, and all life – spiritual – physical – intellectual – is one. God doesn't show up on Sundays and disappear the rest of the week. He Always One. He is the ground. He is One.

Deuteronomy 6:5
14 May 2020

Many acknowledged the greatness of the God of Israel and even respected Him. Nebuchadnezzar and Darius did so. Moses' father-in-law, Jethro, blessed God as recorded in Exodus 18:10-11, but He didn't go beyond that to loving God. I don't know that we could even say that Moses loved God for all the time he spent with Him before we have the commandment of this verse. It's a brave one who will do that at any time, but even moreso if he has not been bidden to do so. We know from verse 1 of this chapter that this a commandment of God from God given to Moses to teach the people.

Loving God is a giant leap forward from fearing or even worshipping God. It goes even beyond the faith of Abraham when Abraham believed God and it was reckoned to him as righteousness. God calls for love as soon as He has told His people who He is and what His nature is. Jesus takes this rather than the statement in the verse before as His starting point for understanding the commandments of God. Doing this builds on fear and worship, but it is also the true way to fear and worship.

Interestingly, God tells us to love our neighbor as ourselves (Leviticus 19:18) before He tells us to love Him. In Exodus 20:6 God talks about people loving Him. The only other time after that He mentions anyone loving Him before this is in the preceding chapter (5:10) where He mentions in passing those who love Him. Neither was a commandment, but only a statement. Here, we get the imperative.

This is connected with the preceding verse by an "and". In other words, verse 5 goes in conjunction with verse 4. You can't take them apart and have them "each sold separately" as advertisers used to say about their products (so you wouldn't get the idea that you got every kind of variety of a toy or widget all at the same time for the price of one). This goes along with God being who He is. It's the logical conclusion and next step to understanding. To know God is to love Him. You can know about Him and possibly not love Him, but you cannot know Him and not love Him.

He says you shall do this. Shall, to me at least, has always carried with the idea of doing something by right, of an oughtness to the doing of it. This is not just something you will do as though it was a simple forecast or prediction of your behavior, but something that you will do because you are supposed to do it. It's right to do it, and it will be done for that very reason.

After you've heard (verse 4), you love.

Love is one of those words that has so many meanings and

connotations. The Greeks had their four words – eros (physical love), philos (brotherly love), storge (family or blood love) and agape (the highest kind of God love). I don't know as much about the Hebrews, but they gave us one of the great love poems of the ancient world, the Song Of Solomon, showing that they certainly understood that physical beauty attraction kind of love. Even Snoopy borrowed from the Song to write to his sweetheart, and he felt that Solomon would understand his using some of his words.

Earlier in the Old Testament before we got to this point it had spoken of loving a child and loving a spouse. Those are usually natural responses or else ones dictated by relationships freely entered into, but this is different. Loving God. That seems almost as impossible as loving Mt. Everest. He is so big, and we are so little, that where would the love be?

Doesn't matter what it seems like. God tells us to do it. It's one of those things that you acquire a perspective for in the doing of it, and not always before.

Love Yahweh your God. He is a person. Only a person can be loved. A think can be regarded as a matter of importance in someone's life, but it can't be love, because in order to be loved there has to be the possibility of a mutual relationship. The one you love has to be able to love you back. If they don't you have a case of unrequited love, but then that can become adoration or adulation. It is the closing of the circuit between the two that makes it love. It is the mutuality of it that does it.

The One we love has a name because He is a person. A name always signifies personality. It is never merely a label. God is capable of returning our love because He's the one who loved first. Sometimes two people will hold back on a relationship or discussion by tossing the "you first" ball back and forth. Somebody has to be first. God is always first because He made us. Now, it's up to us to go on. We are not merely second, though, as though what we does were less important. We love God in such a way that we show that we have gotten who and what God is and how He operates, and we want to operate on that same level.

God is love, so it's natural that someone who wants to deal with Him would deal with Him in love. They would love Him.

Love is not merely focusing emotion on someone else. It's not looking at them hungrily as a source of filling us up emotionally. Love is not about ourselves. It's not about what we want even though the songs are full of wanting and needing. To love is to give. It is to be positive always in the direction and relationship with the other. Loving God is the perfect way to understand the nature of love. When we love Him first as we should, there is no problem in transferring the concept over to loving people.

People are somewhat confused at times about what it means to love God, though. I think that's because this is one of those things we are told to do without being given any steps as to how to carry it out. I believe that we're not given steps because if we had steps we'd concentrate on the steps and come to regard them as a checklist rather than as motivations. So, we're told to love God. The degree to which we do that occupies the rest of this verse, but let's think, in a totally inadequate way, of what it means to love God. We are not going to be able to be exhaustive, but we will make enough points so that there will be no doubt as to what we're talking about. We won't be able to tell everyone how to do it, but we will know that it can be done and the level to which we are to pursue it.

We love God when we recognize Him as the creator of the universe. That's really what the old covenant Sabbath day observance was all about. It wasn't just an enforced rest, but a reminder that God had worked and then rested. Jesus called us into God's own rest. Love recognizes what God has done and the worth of what He has done and His own worth for having done it.

We love God when we love Jesus. It's definitely a love me, love my Son sort of arrangement as John points out in I John 2. We love Jesus when we love one another and when we love the world, not with a love on its level, but with a God-so-loved-the-world kind of love. We are called to love on all levels. When we love the fellow Saints in the church, we are living up to our responsibility to them as our brothers and sisters. When we love the world, we are doing evangelism. When we do service, we are doing things to Jesus.

We love God when we mirror His personality and love. We are to be mimics, not to poke fun or get adulation, but because that's the way to be. When we do what we see Jesus doing, we love God.

We love God when we get into His covenant and stay on and work for His team. No one has to be on the outside. In the world sometimes people unjustly draw lines in the sand forcing us to choose them. They don't have the right to do that. Only God has a right to demand that someone choose Him. We have love relationships where, once we enter into them, we are bound to love, but no one, unless they're in an old fashioned type society where the family demands a marriage with another family even has to get married. That's a freely entered into vow, but once the vow is made the freedom is over. There's no freedom ever to not love God. There is freedom to obey or disobey, but everyone must love God, and when they do not they will lose out forever unless they repent in time.

We love God when we listen to what He says and do it as He says to do it. When people do that to us it is gratifying, but how much more when these are the words of God who knows the absolute truth and right of everything and who gives us all the we need to accomplish that.

We love God when we acknowledge Him as the greatest of all. This is the only way we can love Him. To regard Him as anything other than or less than I Am That I Am is to hate God. There are no shades of gray in the love of God.

We love God, not just when we feel overwhelmed in awe of Him, but when we want to get as close to Him as we can get. We want to be with Him all the time. That, of course, is what is coming in heaven. We should want to be that way now. It won't do us good just to wait.

There's not necessarily anything right or wrong about doing any one particular thing I've mentioned above. Not doing one of them wouldn't throw you out on your ear, but you should not have a problem thinking about doing such things. The rest of the verse is about the degree to which we are love God. It is a degree to which we can take no other love or emotion or attachment or devotion of any kind. When we operate at this level of intensity, there won't really be any problem about doing it.

One thing I've noticed when I really get to playing the piano is that the more I let myself go, the more I can do. It is almost playing recklessly, but it opens the door to more heart and connection than playing carefully would do. even if a person is not a virtuoso who hits every note with exactly the right intensity at exactly the right time without missing a note or a beat, playing with and from the heart is the most important thing. I'd rather hear a child whose heart was into loving Jesus play "Jesus Loves Me" with every other note a mistake than to hear it played perfectly without any heart.

People will say, "Give it all you got." The problem is that we often don't know what all we have. In this context it doesn't mean to stop and take an inventory, but that whatever comes to your mouth or hand or body to do that can love God, you should do it without pause or calculation. This is not the time or place to weigh things out and make sure you got it "exactly right".

Let's start with the word, "All". We always hold something back for a rainy day. That's why Jesus commented on the widow giving her mite. She threw her umbrella away and went out from the temple not concerned about any storm that might come her way. She showed that nothing was off limits in her life for God to take. We may not give everything we own at every assembly or even at any one ever. One of the lessons of Ananias and Sapphira was that they were not obligated to give everything they made on the transaction (nothing was said about everything they owned by either them or Peter), but they were obligated to be truthful about what they gave. We need to stand before God in truth whenever we stand before Him. These three degrees to which we love God are personal rather than financial alls that we are to love God with.

Your heart is your entire inner landscape. We know it's there, but I don't know that we have explored even our own hearts. We contain more than we have time to tell or work out. That may be one of the things we're doing in heaven. I always like that line at the end of the film, "Babette's Feast", in which it is said that in Paradise you will get to be the artist you were meant to be. There is more to us, and there we'll have eternity for it. Right now, though, we need to adopt a heart attitude that is totally open to God. There should be no barriers to His entry and operation inside us.

Your soul is your life force and psychology. The heart is the content, the snips and snails or sugar and spice, but the soul is what you do with it. Some people have all kinds of talents that they never employ. I don't just mean to play the piano or paint a picture, but talents to manage resources or help others and so on. I do not have the gifts of mercy or of helps or of service or anything else along those lines. We are all to help others in the church, but there are some people who just have the gift of that. That is the kind of talent (I don't always differentiate between the two words of talent or gift as some teachers did back in the 70s; the point isn't identifying what you have, but using it, something which is forgotten in the nit picking) that is to be brought out into the open. All of your psychological energy is to go into whatever you do to love God.

Your might is all your physical strength. We are not armchair lovers. We have to get up and get out and do that. People like Stephen and Phillip knew what that meant as have all the deacons and non-official workers in the church down through the centuries. It takes effort and energy to help people clean and move and get places. All of that is loving God when we do it unto others in Jesus' name.

I don't know how much of this sunk in or if it was merely this testimony to what God wanted that rested in the record until Jesus came along and demonstrated it and then pointed us to go to it, but from this verse alone we can know that the end of the law is not doing the law, but loving God. Those who rightly love Him will never do any of the sins that are pointed out in the law, not because they'll be such great folks, but because they are doing the all kind of love that always excludes sin.

Leviticus 19:18
19 May 2021

For some reason I never worked through this verse at a Saturday morning session of our journaling group. There is a chart laid out for the entire year, and we just take the readings for the day and choose something out of them to journal on. Either it didn't happen that we covered this any time I journaled, or, since I've been doing it for 14 years now, I must have had other scriptures that jumped out at me on those days when this passage was on the chart. Anyway, rather than waiting for February 12, 2022, the next time this passage would come up in the rotation (and there is no guarantee that I would be able to be there), I'm going to write on it now to include it with this book.

This is second commandment that Jesus said was greatest. He never said that of any others in the Gospels. God and others are to be our two reference points.

The verse comes in the middle of what many people regard as the driest book of the entire Bible. I've had several people tell me over the years that this is a book they either don't read or don't want to read. If you get hold of it, though, it explains how the sacrifice of Jesus works for us. It also offers some strong teachings that we need, especially here. This verse makes four points. It is the third of those which Jesus cites and builds on, but then He can make a bigger whole out of any part because He knows the very center of every principle and statement. He doesn't quote the first part of the verse, but it would be good for us to look at it and place the whole thing in an even greater perspective with the conclusion of the verse.

1. You are not to take vengeance.

Revenge almost seems to be a right to many people. You did that to me. I have a right to do this to you. Even evil people often expect it, and expecting it they have strategies figured out to either sidestep it or use it for their advantage.

This does not mean that there should be no retributive punishment for things. That is part of the moral fabric of the universe. He who kills a man shall have his blood shed. That's not vengeance. That's justice. The fact that at one time the family avenger of blood dealt out the execution doesn't mean that the execution was not justified. Even that, in the Jewish system, was only subsequent to the judging of the case if the killer could get to a city of refuge. The implication of the scripture, too, is that if he doesn't make it to the city (which is his responsibility, not the responsibility of the state) and the avenger of blood catches him, he does have a right to execute him. That, however, is a separate issue dealing with justice.

This is a case stemming not from objective right or wrong, but from your own interests which decree that something should be done to someone because they did something to you. That's vengeance. It is not the application of a principle of law or righteousness, but of dealing out retribution for your own reception of an offense.

There have been a lot of Westerns made with a revenge motif. I don't think I ever saw one where at the end of it I felt that right had been done. A crime had been committed against the revenger or his family, but his vigilante action never seems to be satisfying. The best of those pictures that I've seen is the Gregory Peck film, "The Bravados". Not to give anything away, but he learned the hard way that his vengeance was wrong. "The Oxbow Incident" with Henry Fonda is almost the textbook study of what's wrong with mob violence which is another form of vengeance without law.

God isn't telling us to leave vengeance out of the picture because he wants to thwart us, but because he wants us to be at peace. I know we can't stand it that that other person has "gotten away" with what they did. I know it seems like stomping on a person who has wronged you or someone you love seems like it would give you an infinite amount of peace, but the moment they died (vengeance usually seeks to do the ultimate), the avalanche of guilt would come on you unless your conscience has been totally seared. Then it would come on you on judgment day. Even the pagan Greeks knew that.

In the famous Oresteian myth cycle of stories, Clytemnestra murdered her husband, Agamemnon because he had offered her daughter, Iphigenia, as a human sacrifice on the way to Troy. In turn her children, Electra and Orestes murdered her, and they then fled before the Nemesis and the Furies. That was a pagan story, and the pagans knew vengeance didn't work. You don't balance the books that way. You only perpetuate the wrong you are against.

Now, God knows much better than the Greeks ever did that this way is the way of tragedy, and He tries to keep us from experiencing it.

Before leaving this, we need to understand that these people we are not wreaking vengeance on are not going to go unpunished. We need to step back to let God take care of them. He can do more than we could ever do, but even the possibility of our delight at God crushing the miscreants isn't the issue. It is that the wisdom of God deals with these people to the exact degree that it needs to deal with them with. We don't have that wisdom so we might exact too much or not enough.

2. You are not to bear a grudge against any of the children of your people.

Oh, come on! At least leave me that!

A grudge is something like an itch. You have to scratch it, but in scratch it, rather than healing yourself, you open yourself to infection. I've had a lot of skin issues over my life and know how hard refraining from scratching can be. This is even worse.

A grudge means an assessment of guilt laid against someone. It's saying that they are eternally wrong and that you have a right to hold it against them. Holding it against them, though, closes off the possibility of love in the next phrase. That's one reason why you shouldn't carry it around with you. Another is that it will weigh you down.

Still, even in joking, Christians say, "You won't know when, but you'll know why." I think there are some people you could joke with in that way, but such joking is not the wisest thing to do.

This section shows up how difficult the path that God is calling us to is, but it also shows that this is the way to satisfaction.

The only way not to bear a grudge is to forgive. That is to release the person from what they have done. It doesn't mean that they didn't do it or that it didn't cause damage, but that they are released. The world doesn't understand that. We should. Like the fellow forgiven his millions in the parable, we are to pass forgiveness on to someone who just owes us a ten. Forgiveness is supposed to be catching. Imagine if the fellow in the parable had forgiven his debtor who then went out and forgave his debtor who owed him a dime. You'd have had a chain reaction of something so far removed from the system and practices of the world that people who have taken notice.

I don't think that he means that we can bear grudges against outsiders here, but that your own people are the hardest to forgive because you expect the outsiders to be up to no good, and you expect your people to be up to good and nothing but good, but they're not always that.

These are people we have to live with. How can we live with someone with a wall of strife between us? We can't. God is not just setting impossibly high standards, but is telling us what will work and what won't work. We don't have to figure it out for ourselves. Scripture means that there doesn't have to be trial and error about spiritual things. We know because we've been told. It's been totally revealed to us.

In the love chapter of I Corinthians 13 Paul told us that love doesn't keep a record of wrongs suffered. That's what it means to not bear a grudge. You don't even have it written down where you will remember to do something about it. You don't keep the record. I've found, particularly in recent years, that if I don't write it down, I forget it. That can be bad about appointments I need to keep, but it's great about this. Don't write it down in your heart, and you won't keep it.

3. Love your neighbor as yourself

This is where I know I will not say enough, but in working

through this I hope to say some things that will be of value to myself and to my readers.

You should do this. It's not just a serving suggestion. It's a command from God to all men for all time. Jesus didn't make it or ratify it; He merely reminded us of it. Some people have said that in the church we need more reminding than being told things.

Forgiveness alone is not the root that will enable you to do the first two parts of this verse. Loving your neighbor is the antidote to vengeance and the corrective of the grudge.

Love is such a big word that we hardly don't know what it means half the time. Love is not what is in your interest, but what is in the interest of others. It's not about protecting yourself, but about enlarging others.

Love is always a positive thing. It is always a deliberate thing. It's never inadvertent. You might inadvertently do someone a kindness, but you can't inadvertently love them. You have to mean it because love does not depend on the other's reception, but on your giving.

That last phrase may be enough to work on in considering this concept. We want to know that something will work out before we undertake it. We want to know that it is actually possible. If conventional wisdom says it is not, then we are likely to abandon it. Those who made great discoveries persisted until they found what they were looking for. I'm not saying that everyone who did, but that those who did find never did so first time at bat, other than maybe Fleming who found penicillin in a petri dish without looking for it.

Popular music culture is filled with songs of unrequited love. Those were largely the bulk of the ballads brought over from England which eventually turned into the country music of America. The singer bemoans the fact that the girl didn't love him back. If that was the ultimate reality, God would really be belting one out. The thing about love is not whether it is received or not, but about whether it is given or not. Someone may not receive it, but if you give it, you receive the benefit of having given. It does something to you inside.

God is wanting us to love our neighbor. They're the hardest to love. It's easy to "love" someone you'll never meet. You can think all sorts of good thoughts to and about them, but that's not really love. The people we know are the people who challenge us. They are the only ones we can really love. Remember that Jesus defined the neighbor as not someone who has a house near your house, but as someone who, regardless of where they "live", is where you are. That's why Fred Rodgers could reach out across the airwaves and call his viewers, "Neighbors". They really were his neighbors, even if they never met him face to face because His love was expressed to them over the air waves.

He is an example of love sent out without regard to who might or might not receive it.

We are not to define our love for the neighbor by our willingness to love, but by the love we feel for ourselves. I know that there are disturbed people who can't love themselves, but they are not the norm, nor are they the ones Jesus is referring to. We all want our own comfort, our own healing, our own good feelings, our own relationships. Remember that love is a word of relationship, not of things. It is about those we are in fellowship with. To be in isolation is one of the worst things that can happen to a person. In our society today someone can be alone in a crowd. I think there was a song written about that years ago, but I don't know what it was called or who wrote it.

We take care of ourselves. We are to take care of our neighbors. This, of course, is only possible when we have first loved God. Putting people ahead of God will not do you or the people any good. That's why the girlfriend who worships a boyfriend at the cost of all truth and other relationships is doomed for trouble. That's not the only example I could give of inordinate love, but you get the picture.

When we look at other people in the same way that we look at ourselves, we begin to get the picture. Too often people place themselves in a separate category from the rest of the world. They're like an old European saying I read of once - First, I come. Then, I come again. And you, you don't come for a long time.

We are all creatures before God. In the church, we are all Saints sanctified by the blood of Jesus. No one got more blood than someone else. We all got the complete absolute cleansing which freed us from sin and guilt and opened the way to fellowship with God. When we realize that what is true of us is true of others as well, we have a proper ground for loving. If we are any in the least superior, love is probably not going to be love.

4. I am Yahweh

The reason for all of this is that the one speaking to us is Yahweh. He is the I Am That I Am. He is the creator and redeemer. He is the judge. He is over all.

We want a good reason for doing something we really don't want to do. After all, there are some neighbors who haven't been the least bit neighborly, so couldn't we just ignore them or pass them by like the priest and Levite did in the parable about the beaten up man on the Jericho road? They didn't beat him up? They didn't cause him harm? They just didn't help him. It is that not helping him which is unlove. And, it is ungodly.

Everything is to be in accordance with God. That's why in my book, The Learning Tree, I began all understanding of the teaching of the Bible with the doctrine of God. Actually, I didn't think that up. It's inherent in the word all the way through.

All right. It may be time to duck on this next one.

Is Yahweh, your God, the God of your love, or is He only the God of your salvation? Only you can answer this question because only you can love your neighbor as yourself. No one else can love your neighbor in accord with your person. That makes you unique and significant. Even though God so loved the world, both He and the world are waiting for you to love. That's why Jesus put this as the second great commandment like the first. To love is to live in accord with the character of God.

Genesis 15:6
6 January 2018

This is an eternal principle for all people in all places at all times. We wouldn't know that we could do it if Paul hadn't told us in Romans 4. Without the New Testament testimony all of these things might have been what Abraham did, what Noah did, what Moses did and nothing more. Here we have something we can all do.

I don't do sacrifices like Adam. I don't build an ark like Noah. I don't have a child at 100 like Abraham. But, I do have faith.

Faith comes in the stream of things. In this chapter we see the following stream: God comes to Abraham > God speaks to Abraham > Abraham questions God > God corrects Abraham > God directs Abraham to the stars as an illustration.

Faith never comes until after we have heard from God. Faith follows God; it doesn't precede Him. You believe on the basis of what God has said or done. You cannot believe on any other basis.

Faith never starts things off, but faith finishes them. It is leaning on God. You can't lean on something that is not there. Faith is always your declaration that God is there and that He can bear your weight. We sometimes try to bear our own weight or find someone to bear it. God bears it all the way.

Then, after all this preceding, he believed. If most people said to us what God said to Abraham, we would say in a very sarcastic voice, "Right." Faith doesn't just speak. It acts and it does so after it has examined everything available to it. I don't mean that it understands or explains everything, but that it knows what it is that is being believed. It doesn't make snap judgments. It doesn't do impulse purchases. This is why we need to fully inform people and ourselves regarding Jesus and God.

He believed. Abraham did this. It was an action, not a work, but an action. People who say, "You don't do anything to be saved," are wrong. When the question in scripture came, "What must I do to be saved," no one ever said, "Nothing."

In believing he gave up every reservation and bought into everything God said. Faith has no shades. It's belief or unbelief. Greater faith is not a degree, but a number. It's believing more than 6 unbelievable things before breakfast. It's believing every thing which the world says is unbelievable about God. Faith testifies that God always knows best. It freely acknowledges that we do not know better than God, something which, of course, doesn't work.

He believed. It was done. It was a past event from author Moses' standpoint. Faith needs to be in our past, but it needs to stay in our present. That's the only way it will get us to God's future.

He believed in the Yahweh. All of his believing went into God. There was no doubt left. That didn't mean that Abraham was infallible. He took Hagar after this. He tried to "help" God.

We can't look at the calendar when it comes to believing God. God is the I Am. He is not confined to any date. It's not that we put our faith in the Lord, but that we put ourselves there. We have to be **in** Him. In is a specific preposition. There is a difference between in and out.

Abraham put his future in the Lord. He put his trust in the Lord. He put his family in the Lord. Do we really think we can do a better job that the Lord can?

Keep this in mind: Abraham had no word about what faith would do for him before he believed. It was only what God would do for him. He would have a child from his own body. He would have infinite descendants that included not only the genetic progeny of Isaac, but spiritual progeny including us as well.

And God added to what Abraham did. God is a value-adding God. He adds, not in terms of bank account or quality of life, but in terms of eternity. Like the woman forgets the pains of childbirth when she has the child, we will forget this life. Everything will fade away before the joy of heaven. I could name specifics, but I won't have them there, so I'll give them up here.

God looks at faith and says that He will count that righteousness for us, whether we can ever completely do righteousness
s (and that's' the only way it can be done – 100%) or not. Faith puts us in God, and when we are there, God does   something with us that we could not do with ourselves.

He reckoned. God did the reckoning. God only. We didn't help. God did it. This is not what our faith did, but what God did with our faith. Faith is not the cause, but the occasion. God was free to act or not act on faith.

Our faith, though, depends on God, not on what God will do with it.

Reckon is an accounting term. It is to accept one thing for another. God demanded absolutely righteousness. Abraham was never absolutely righteous. God said that Abraham's faith would be counted as righteousness, not that it would be righteousness. It was on the basis of God's will, not Abraham's. Abraham never willed righteousness for himself. We can't, either. We know now that's how it works, and we can take advantage of it, but Abraham didn't know. He just believed. It was pure belief in God with no preconceived notions.

Faith needs to be single and simple. There can be nothing but

God in it - none of us in it at all. That's challenging.

God charged this to Abraham's account. He put it there where Abraham could draw on it. God made righteousness - which is needed to approach God - available to Abraham (and us).

Righteousness - it is to be legally correct in every relationship. The most important relationship is with God.

God made Abraham a straight line so Abraham could be parallel to God and in faith, to an extent, merge with God. He was not merely called righteous, but reckoned righteous meaning that he was righteous. Absolutely straight, always equidistant in his relationship to God, going the same direction to the same destination as God.

Without righteousness we would be uncomfortable before God. We wouldn't be able to stand in His presence. We wouldn't want to be around Him.

Righteousness changes our entire present, life, focus, future. Abraham was something different from this point forward. So are we. This is a constitutional change. It is not designed to be a temporary arrangement. God wants righteous to be for always. It doesn't say that we can't lose it, but that we have it. God straightens things out for us, and we can build our house on that ground. In all things, God has the final word.

Abraham got this. We can get it. How?

Do what Abraham did.

Genesis 3:22
2 January 2021

God and man. Here we have the definition of them and where they intersect, so to speak, and where they differ. This is something which stands.

God was always this. He was always what He was. He is the only ever legitimate tautology. All others are variations and variations and outright exclusions from categories they pretend to.

Man became this, and the this was a being who knew information that he didn't know before. He didn't change his nature, but his awareness. There is no mention of the word "nature" at all with regard to this story as set forth in Genesis. In the New American Standard Version, the word, nature, doesn't even appear until the New Testament. There's no translation of any word as "nature" in the King James Version at all. If a nature shift was involved here, God didn't mention it, and what is not mentioned is not for our concern. People can misconstrue the slogan, "Where the scriptures are silent we are silent," but there is no way a doctrine of a sin nature or even of some kind of specific human nature can be built out of a void. Speculation may explain some things, but an explanation is not a revelation, and we don't have to accept one.

Perception is not everything, but it is much, and it can govern your life and your action. The night before doing this entry we watched "The Russians Are Coming! The Russians Are Coming!" The film is over 50 years old, and the cold war has gone, at least as it was then, but it still speaks to us. The opening image is of an eyeball. It turns out to be the captain of a Russian submarine staring at America through the periscope. I had never noticed that before, but it seems like all the way through the film, as much as being a comic take on the cold war, it is about how perceptions govern everyone. People went crazy, not because there was any real danger, but because they perceived that there was danger. Perceptions, however, do not carry the weight of either reality or revelation.

I first learned about perception as a small child. I don't know how old I was, but for some reason I approached our house from the other side of the street and from the opposite direction that I normally walked in, and it almost looked like it was a different street. I went to the right house. I didn't get confused, but it all looked different. Filmmakers have even done that. They've had one Western town set and simply by shooting from the other end of the street it looks like a different town. (They probably change a few signs, but that may be all.)

We have got to get away from what we perceive in our brain and go by what we receive from the Lord. Adam and Eve forgot to do that. The fruit "looked good" (3:6), and the woman took it and ate it. She was no longer acting on God's word, and when the man ate it, he knew full well what he was doing as Paul testifies in I Timothy 2:14. He didn't even misperceive. He just disobeyed.

The Lord God is Yahweh Elohim if we really put the names correctly (very few English translations do). His name was first given in 2:4. He is the same being with many names and designations. Also, I don't believe in the authorship theory which regards Genesis as a synthesis between a Yahweh (or Jehovah) source and an Elohim source, as though it were a synthetic work rather than the Holy Spirit inspired book written by Moses which it is. If there is what seems to be a difference it is because it is the same sort of thing we do where we tell a story in quick summary and then go back and fill in the details in a second telling.

There is only one Yahweh Elohim. Actually, there's only one Elohim, even though pretenders use that title which is the class name of God (He's the only one in the class). Saying Yahweh Elohim really keeps us from confusion or misidentification. We will never have any other god before or beside or in place of Yahweh Elohim if we have Him.

He said this. To whom? To Himself? I don't think God is speaking directly to Adam. God did say it, however, so we could know it. God speaks constantly through the scriptures. I don't ever remember a time where God "thought" something. I just now did a quick run through of my concordance, and I can't find a place where it says God thought anything. I suppose there could be other synonyms to describe God thinking, but I can't remember one. We know there are things in the mind of the Lord that we don't know, but in the Bible He always speaks because the Bible is a book of revelation, not of cogitation. He always speaks. The mind and counsels are referred to, but we have no clue as to what might be in there and anything specific is spoken. Either Adam heard this and passed it down or it was revealed directly to Moses when he was under inspiration to write this. We don't know. What we do know is that God said it.

Behold is always a strong word in the mouth of God or Jesus or by the word of the Holy Spirit. God remarks on man's sin here. Jesus remarked on faith when He saw it. Which would you rather God remark on in you?

This didn't just happen. It was known by God. Nothing we do is **not** known by God.

The man here is not demeaning. Adam's name means man. Some people say that at times about family members referring to the son or the daughter or the like.

God made the man, but He didn't abandon or discard him over this. He didn't throw the clay away, as a song sung by the Lesters proclaims.

The man has become like one of us. It doesn't mean that man became God, but that he became like God in a way that he had not been like Him before. God is a knowing begin. He knows all things. Man is limited in being and in knowledge, but at this point he knew what he had not known before. His knowledge was expanding.

The man was created in the image of God to begin with, but he was striving to take the prerogative of God to know all things. God probably knows things He wishes He didn't know. He wants to spare us that, but we have to be know-it-alls at times. How much better to know what you're told to know.

People can get into trouble even in this world when they know what they're not supposed to know. Then, the villain has to kill them. God doesn't kill here, but He controls. Man had aspired to knowledge and attainted at least differential knowledge, but he was not to achieve eternity at the same time.

Us is a word about the plurality of God. The –im ending on Elohim states that every time. Even without the New Testament we would have known that God was single, but in some kind of multiple way.

Keep this clear. God (nor Moses in reporting this) does not say that Adam became God or even became a god in one particular. Before, man had only known good. Now he knew, experientially, evil. It was not all possible evil, but he knew that there were things that we not good. Knowing that there is even one upsets the entire apple cart. It didn't have to be that way. We are not determined. We can choose. The problem comes in choosing the wrong when you didn't have to.

Sometimes, we think we're doing the right thing, and then the second we do something, we know it's wrong. That's happened to me when I've taken the wrong exit on the freeway which I could not back out of or reroute away from immediately. The moment I was on the wrong road, I knew I was on the wrong road. That's a non-moral situation, but it's far worse to make the wrong moral choice and end up in judgment for sin.

Adam knew the good before, but now good and evil. We were not intended to know evil. No parent intends that his child should know the wrong with the possible exception of a criminal or sociopath. Even those often want their child to better than they were. Mickey Rooney's criminal brother in "Boy's Town" knew that he had already chosen the wrong road with all its consequences (he didn't think he could repent), but he didn't want his brother to go down that road, so he gets Father Flanagan to take him on. I don't know if that was a real story or just one made up for the movie and put into a real setting, but it doesn't matter because it is true to people and illustrates the point.

To know evil is to be able to define it. It's more than saying, "I'll know it when I see it." Once you learn evil you always know it before you see it. To define is to be, in a limited way, in participation with it.

Man is not limitless in his ability. God kept him from stretching his hand out to the tree of life. That remains for us in Paradise, but not until then.

To stretch out is to act. Man is an acting being, not a sedentary stone. He is not to take also from the tree of life and eat it.

I was trying to figure out whether eat was a one time occurrence or an ongoing occurrence, but I couldn't determine it from the analytical lexicon I had. So I tried to find out the tense of stretch out. It appears to be simply future, so I don't know whether this was something Adam would have done one time like a vaccination and been in life from then on or if he had to continually eat from it, and as long as he ate he would be alive. There may be a commentator that defines it, but I just wanted to see if I could do some from the text itself, and my Hebrew knowledge being limited pretty much to only being able to look up words, I couldn't. So, while anything I might say could be only a conjecture, I'll take a stab at it. The bottom line is the same whether it was a one time eating or an ongoing eating.

It doesn't say that he had eaten from this before. Maybe he didn't need to because as long as he didn't eat of the tree of knowledge he would stay on. In that case, the tree of life might be an antidote, but it was one God was not willing to use at that time. He couldn't overcome his sin simply by eating like Alice eating from the two sides of the mushroom until she got to be the size she wanted to be. I don't think though, that it was an antidote. It is something that can be taken once the sin is dealt for, but to take of it now would be to enfranchise the sin and might even be taken as approving of sin. Like Hamlet's step-father, Adam couldn't partake of the fruits of his sin and be free of the guilt of it. The guilt required more.

These trees are what they produce – knowledge and life. Once having eaten he would have lived forever, but without Jesus it would have been like the early Twilight Zone episode where the fellow got the gift of not being able to die and then, having committed a murder, thinking he was immune to all consequences, was given a life sentence. Then, the gift became a curse because he couldn't be freed from prison by death.

Adam threw away living forever at that time. Curiosity killed the man, and satisfaction left it at that.

Man is in the image of God. he knows the categories God knows, but when it comes to eternal life, he has to wait for Jesus. We now have all three. All we need is heaven, and that's coming.

TWO CAMPS

GOD IS BEGINNING TO DEAL WITH JACOB DIRECTLY. That is the turning point of his entire story. Without it, there is no story. God's dealings with us are what make our story, also.

Jacob was aware of angels. Unlike some of us, he had seen them to know them when he saw them again. Twenty years before he had seen the ladder they climbed on connecting heaven and earth. Now he sees the angels of God on earth encamped around his own camp.

Before, they had been going back and forth to the throne and the earth. Now they are angel hosts to defend him in the coming contest.

At Bethel he saw them in a dream. Here, they appeared to him when waking as if yet stronger assurance.

He saw this. It was actual sensory perception, not something that took place in his mind's eye.

In the angels he discerned the encampment of God. They were God's camp. The angels weren't powerful independent beings. Their power only worked from God.

The help of God is powerful and real. It is not all in our heads or in a once upon a time story book.

Mahanaim is a Hebrew word in the plural which means camps or two hosts. It became the proper name of a town beyond Jordan no the borders of Gad and Manasseh. It later became a Levitical town.

It is a double camp or double host, so called because the host of God joined his host as a safeguard. Jacob's own company was matched by another. This was heartening because soon his own camp would be split because of fear.

This is God's camp and ours combined together against the world. We need the combination to have the full strength necessary for what we are dealing with. God can do what He needs to do alone, but we can't do what we need to do without Him.

Jacob was able to take on what came his way because he was aligned with the camp of God even though he didn't always think he could.

> ➢ Meeting with Esau.
> ➢ Resettlement

> ➤ Loss of Joseph
> ➤ Anguish over Benjamin
> ➤ Recovery of all.

Taking the information from Genesis, there are other applications to be made from this story. In every case we have to choose what camp we are going to be aligned with.

I.   Living on your own (1 camp)
       Vs
       Life with God (having two camps)
       In this choice we don't just half as many camps, we get zero resources. To be on your own in the universe is scarier than crossing Jurassic World with nothing but the clothes on your back.

II.   You have to change your address.
       You can't expect to get the blessings of God while living the life of the world. You have to get all the way into the land to get this camp.

III.   Outside God's camp is danger.
       There is a third camp there. It will always be against you, never for you.
       In the end every other ally will desert you when you face difficulty.
       The camp is about warfare. We are all in a warfare whether we want to be or not. This is a base camp. You decide what it is a base for (yourself or God; these are the only two deities we ultimately must choose between).
       You decide who is your captain. It would be good to choose the God of the Battle Lines, the Lord of your own army's ranks (see I Samuel 17:45).

IV.   It devolves down to the difference between living
       FOR the moment (making the moment all our own)
       or
       IN the moment (what God wants)

When we live IN the moment it doesn't matter what the moment is. This is not stoic or ascetic detachment, but reality.
       You have to choose whether you think it's necessary or not.
       There is, however a problem here. I would call it the naïveté of advocacy. This consists of thinking that if people just "see" something

they'll change. There are two problems with that view.
1.   The majority NEVER "see" it.
2.   The majority of those who do "SEE" it think that seeing is enough.

Advocacy must persuade. In the world this is done through manipulation. In the spiritual realm this is accomplished, not by our rhetoric, but by the work of the Holy Spirit on the heart.

One final note: I have camped out in tents only a few times, once in Yosemite and at a couple of parks in Southern California. I've known what it is to feel the isolation away from home and from others. Don't let that happen to you eternally.

Numbers 16:5
24 February 2018

What they were supposed to be, we are. That's why this passage is important to us.

These three things were revealed by God in the midst of the rebellion. He doesn't define the counterfeit, but the true, and He does this in the mist of testing and trying and judging unrighteousness. His truth is marching on. He is always judging these things, but He is also always wanting to find faithfulness and reward it.

Moses is saying this to the people of Korah. They were Levites who were not content to be helpers. They had to be chiefs. I wonder if they thought through the fact that in order to be God's representatives, God would have to accept them or if they thought that they were going to define and control God for the people. Under such circumstances do such people even believe there is a God. In verse 3 they saw Moses and Aaron as usurpers of the rights of God, and they were going to do right by God. How many times do rebels begin with such talk? Do they really think it? Or are they just saying such things to dupe the people into following them?

Moses sets the date: tomorrow morning. Death is normally a pop quiz, but here it's scheduled open book. I believe the time is given so they might repent even though it's not stated as such. They have one night in which to think this through. He doesn't offer repentance, but if they had repented, I believe God would have treated them as He did Ahab and Nineveh, neither one of which had been given an opportunity of repentance from God. The judgment hadn't yet been pronounced as it was in the case of the nation two chapters earlier where they tried to repent about their decision to go along with the fearful 10 spies after they saw what God did to them. In their case, judgment had been pronounced, and the season for repentance was over. Even though repentance hadn't been "granted" as a system, I believe God responds to it, as long as it comes **before** judgment. Whatever we do, it has to be done now, and it has to be done quickly.

The Lord - Yahweh - is going to show this. Keep in mind through all of these entries that Yahweh is not a title or designation; it is the personal name of God. God defines His priests and ministers. The difference in the New Testament is that we can seek for it where it was rigid in the Old Testament, but I think there were still ways for people to serve God on their own initiative, provided they did so within God's parameters and didn't ignore them as Uzzah did.

The woman who made room for Elisha served God in that way. So did Hannah in giving God Samuel her son. Some of the judges seem to have done things that they were not specifically told to do by God. At least we have no record, for example, of Ehud being told to stab Eglon, the king of Moab, with his left hand. In Judges 3:16 Ehud is given the credit for making and positioning the sword. Now, I'm not saying that we should form a Jesus Hit Squad, but that sort of extreme example shows that ministry to God is possible without being "in power". The judges don't seem to have had that kind of power. The only time someone tried to make it into a hereditary office like that of a king, he, Abimelech, lost his life.

We are now in the talent mode where we are to mobilize and invest what we have from God. Basically, what God is saying bout Aaron as priest here, He also says about the Christian who is also a priest with direct access to God.

Here, God is going to show three things about His priest.

1. The priest is one who is His (i.e. He belongs to God).

God defines this always. Here He defined it by His choice of Aaron. For more on that, see chapter 17 about Aaron's rod in which the choice of Aaron is confirmed by the miracle of God. Now God defines things by who believes. This is because God has opened the door to all.

We should want to be His. Did Korah's people really want to be God's? If they did, they would have done it God's way, not theirs. With God it was, "Love me; love my priest." They could still have come to God. They just would have had to do it through Aaron. Why did that stick in their craw?

To be God's is a great thing. Common things acquire great value by being owned by great people. A handkerchief owned by Abraham Lincoln, make that even half a handkerchief, would be worth more than a hundred hand made quilts (or so I think). And, if you could extract his DNA from where he had wiped his brow in the sun...

Our value increases by our being God's. We belong to God by right of purchase from I Corinthians 6:19-20. Belonging means to be owned by to be part of something, to be all in outright. When we are just our own, it's hardly anything. The way to be valuable and to be God's, then, is to do it God's way.

2. The priest is one who is holy.

He is set apart, dedicated, different. There are many other parts to this definition, but these are enough to set forth what we need to consider here.

To be set apart for God means we can't be for ourselves. The will to power the Korahites were trying to express would have been out of the picture if they had been really holy. Holy is defined by a standard outside yourself. When we are holy, we are outside the common herd. We are not like everyone else who's doing it.

To be dedicated means to be about one thing or one person. Only. No one else can use what is dedicated, and one who is dedicated cannot use themselves for anyone but the one they are dedicated to. Yet, people without handicaps park in handicap spaces. They don't respect the dedication.

To be different is a great burden. I've always been a little eccentric, and I grew up in a family that was not like anyone else I knew. I was thrilled when my close high school fried, Ron, commented on that once. It wasn't just what I thought. It was really so. In this situation, though, to be different is to be unlike the world. The world is going to hell; we are going to heaven. That, just for one, is a great difference to be participating in. Vive le difference!

There is only one way we can be these things. That is for God to make us holy. Holiness is not ever inherent in us. It is never achieved or earned by us. It is always acquired. We have a part in getting it through our belief, but belief doesn't make us holy. It has to be reckoned as righteousness, and we can't do the reckoning – only God can.

3. The priest is one who He (God) brings near to Himself.

The Spy who was going to come in from the cold in the bestselling 60s novel didn't come in because of the injustice of his own side. They were right, but unjust. God is right and just, and we can freely and easily come to him, but we don't have to in some ways. In this instance, He brings us to Him.

We believe, but it is not our believing that does the bringing. The believing tells God we want Him to do the bringing, and He does it.

We need to be brought close to God because to be in ministry is to be under fire. Moses was. Jesus was. Paul was. ETC.

But, it is also to be brought to God. In being brought near to God, all self-effort is out. God does this to us.

Here, it is Aaron, the one God will designate that He has chosen to be His priest. God brought Aaron near by letting him into the holy of holies. In a sense, Moses also is covered because God brought him to the burning bush and the mountain, and He met with him in the tent of meeting.

Being brought near to God is the greatest thing that can happen to you. It signifies that you are in Jesus Christ and totally acceptable to God. Everything will be clear there. We will have full understanding. Every need will be met there. Full fellowship will be there.

God was going to test Korah, but Aaron is the one who was going to be approved.

According to Exodus 19:6 all the Israelites were to be priests. Then, it was narrowed down to those out of the one tribe of Levi. The point of the priest is that he has direct access to God and to people. The New Testament teaches the priesthood of all believers. The Old Testament ideal is not realized. According to Revelation 1:6 we are priests now, not at some unspecified time in the future. That is why this verse has meaning for us now so long after it was written through Moses.

The world will be tested (and found wanting); the Saints will be the approved. We are approved by faith, not by works or merits or successes.

Genesis 6:6
3 January 2015

This is a scripture that has to be taken into account. You cannot bypass it or explain it away. If it is not really true, then what of the rest of scripture can be accounted true?

The foreknowledge of God did not keep Him from creating man. If I knew I was going to regret something that much I wouldn't do it unless I still had a reason for doing it.

God did it anyway. He made man. Why? Not for Himself, but for us.

Still, the Lord was sorry. There's a word that needs investigation. What exactly does it mean? God, who knows all was sorry? God who has all power and could have prevented evil, was sorry? God, who could have just stayed in heaven and become a deist God, was sorry?

God had invested Himself in creation. You don't invest yourself in something without feeling for it and about it. This alone tells us that God is not a deist deity with a clockwork universe. Man is not an "independent" being. God is invested in man. If a pot of sauerkraut was burned and had to be thrown out, I wouldn't feel the least bit of remorse. If a pot of caramel sauce for caramel corn got burned and I couldn't use it, I would be sad, partly because of the waste of the potential, but also because I wouldn't get to partake of the caramel corn.

God wanted to partake of man, so to speak, in fellowship with man. Sin cut that off.

First, it was the sin of disobedience to God. Now it has come to wickedness (verse 5), evil thoughts (verse 5), violence (verse 11), and corrupt ways (verse 12). It is the violence of man to one another that corrupts the earth (verse 13), not littering or pollution or excessive fluorocarbon emissions.

God was sorry, not for what man had done, but for what He Himself had done. He had made man on the earth. God took full responsibility for making man. He is not responsible for what man does, i.e. sin, but He is responsible for controlling, correcting and punishing his creation.

God is the one who made man on the earth. This cuts out chance, any kind of a big bang, even daemons or emanations or demigods creating man. God owns up to it. "I did it," He is saying through Moses' writing.

God had to have told someone this – either Noah or Moses directs as a commentary on this story. This is a fact we would not have known apart from revelation. We couldn't have deduced it from creation. We can understand certain general things about God from creation, but not this specifically.

Man owes his origin to God alone. We were placed on this earth. Science marvels that this is the only place in the solar system which could support "life as we know it". They see it as chance. The scriptures do not.

God created everything for the sole purpose of putting us here. As the moon controls the tides, I believe that everything else in space – galaxies, quasars, stars – you name it, is all there to balance the universe so that we can live in it.

God was grieved in His heart. It's no surprise that God has a center since we have one, and we were made in His image. God is always about the heart. He looks on the heart, not the outward appearance. The physically challenged fellow at the Methodist church who led the VBS I attended there was the one I really learned that lesson from.

God was grieved in His heart. He does not like to be thwarted, not because He's got an ego, but because He really does know better (than we know). Knowing best for everyone and seeing everything take less than best – that would certainly be occasion for grief.

This again shows God's investment in man. When God grieves he has to do something about it. He does two things.

1. Blots out man (verse 7).
2. Has favor for Noah (verse 8).

This is still the two part program of the future. All men will either.

A. Find Grace

or

B. Be blotted out.

Death puts a person out of this world. Hell puts a person out of God's presence altogether.

God will not leave man to his own devices. He will open a door of resolution. He will not again destroy the earth until He has provided a way of escape in Jesus. We don't see any more such world wide cataclysmic prophecies until those of Jesus. the punishment up to His time is always limited to death or exile, but not total earth population annihilation. The next time, though, it will be earth and lost mankind altogether.

Man is tied in to the earth, not as its child, but as a place for living in the flesh. We could not live as we are now in the ocean or in outer space or in the core of the earth.

This verse speaks of God's concern for us. it speaks of His concern for our good. God wants us to be good. he doesn't want us to be bad. He doesn't want us to receive the flood or hell or any of the wars and earthquakes in between. (Those are only interim judgments, not final judgments. Even in disaster movies such as "2012)" there are still people who are left at the end of the day to carry on. It's not all over. We can't even really conceive of it being all over.)

I want a God who is grieved when I sin, not one who is indifferent or unmoved or peeved or outraged. The wrath revealed from heaven in Romans 1:18 is not judgment, but warning. Everything negative from God on this side of heaven is warning.

How many warnings much God give before we get it? How long must He wait to cap it all off? Only He knows.

The grief of God is kept from taking the foreground because of the grace of God. See II Peter 3:9. But, eventually, grace will step aside. God knows when and why that will happen. We are given the opportunity to choose between grieving God and accepting His grace to cover and remove everything that has grieved Him.

That fact that He remembers no more is one of the great facts of God. He will never treat us on the basis of our sins once He has forgiven us! Even the grief of God did not so control Him that He could not save anyone.

God has emotions, but He is not controlled by them. He is controlled by Himself. He is the model of self control. Whatever He does in judgment is not done by the pique of the moment, but it is the settled wisdom of God balancing out all!

This all shows how BIG God is.

Still, people ask why God, who knows everything, would do something that He would be sorry for or repent of or regret?

We sometimes put ourselves in places where our emotions are going to be challenged. That's why people go to teary movies. My favorite is the Ronald Colman 1935 "A Tale Of Two Cities". I know ahead of time that there is going to be a scene in the end where Sydney Carton is talking to the little seamstress who is going to the guillotine with him that day. She recognizes that he is not the man who was condemned, and she asks him why he is doing this. I don't know how many times I've seen it, but when he says, "Because he is my friend," it hits me. It is sorrowful and exalting all at the same time. I know it's going to happen, but I keep watching that movie nevertheless.

I think the fact that God would have known that He was going to cry over this, so to speak, was not something to deter Him. In His case, it was because beyond all this, He could do something about it to redeem it, even though He had to judge it.

Ultimately, God changed His mind about making man, and what He changed His mind to was re-making man. If God can do such a turn about, we can, too. We can change our mind about our self course and turn about to God's course.

Leviticus 1:3
6 February 2016

Here we have the criteria for offering. It was the criteria for both Israel and God. There was no double standard. There could be no New Testament sacrifice without this Old Testament prescription. God keeps His own law in sacrificing Jesus.

The burnt offering is **ALL** God's. The worshipper retains or partakes of none of it. Neither the priest, as prescribed in Numbers 18:10, nor the Levite gets a part of it as they do with some of the sacrifices. We are not told what this offering is for other than that it is for God. It is classified as "atonement" in verse 4 which stands for covering, but it doesn't say what is covered. Purposes are known with the peace offering, the thank offering, the sin offering, the atonement offering, etc. It is significant that the first offering is **just for God**. How many things in our lives are just for God?

This is an offering, a thing given to God. We offer it to Him. He has to accept it in order for it to do us any good.

Not all offerings are acceptable. We are not told the reason why, but God did not accept Cain's offering in Genesis 4:5. I'm not sure it was the things that Cain offered as much as it was Cain and his spirit and attitude that disqualified the offering. No girl would ever accept a proposal offered in anger or with a lot of reservations.

There are places where what is acceptable is spelled out. This is the beginning of them. The kinds of animals, grain kinds and amounts, etc. They are all set forth in precise details. This is important to us because if we understand how God set up the sacrificial system, we'll understand how Jesus fulfills the sacrificial requirements.

This is burnt. It is not destroyed. What it was is consumed. It is used up for God. Fire is applied to it. It is turned into ashes and gases. There is death to the flesh and life for the spirit as a result of the sacrifice.

Fire was one of the four elements of the Greeks. Fire provides warmth, but in this case it is applied in order to change things. It breaks things down, releasing all kinds of gases, etc. It uses oxygen, an indispensable element of the air for life. Sacrifices use what we have in this world for our benefit in another world.

These were from the herd. Only certain animals were acceptable. They had to be clean animals from those defined elsewhere by the fact that they both part the hoof and chew the cud or else clean birds which are specified by name. As far as I know, those are the only two categories from which sacrifices were drawn. There were no sacrifices of fish or insects or any other kinds of creatures. In this case, it's the large scale animals we're dealing with. From the herd tells us that these are the highest most expensive sacrifices. They seem to start there and work down. Verse 5 calls it a bull. I think that's the top you could have offered.

It says twice that he is to offer it - once regarding what it is, once regarding where it is to be offered.

It is a male without defect. As far as I know, only the ashes of the red heifer involve the use of a female animal in any sacerdotal or ritual system of the law. The only other uses of heifers in the Old Testament was when Abraham had to kill one in Genesis 15:9 (an act outside the law of Moses), when a heifer was killed in the situation of an unsolved murder near a town and then when Samuel took one to offer in I Samuel 16:2. None of those were parts of the general sacrificial system, however.

Why a male? We don't know if male animals were created first, but in the case of human beings males came first. People may argue against the "male" element in all of this, but we didn't make it up. God said it. It's His requirement. That sets the tone, not human political reasoning.

The male animal is usually the leader in the herd. No one makes that happen. They're not trained to such dominance. We see it by observation. He is the source of guidance and strength. God wants the leader. If He has that one, He'll have the follower.

There are only two sexes. Jesus was going to be a man. It could even be that this condition was set here so that when Jesus fulfilled it, it would be known to be in synch with God's will. Jesus was a man by classification and by gender.

The male initiates procreation. He is the instigator, the begetter. Both sexes are needed, but when a child is born, it's the man's fault. He stands at the beginning of his generation, and if he is cut off there is at least a measure of his generation that does not follow. .

The male sacrifice is not just the sacrifice of one particular animal. It is the sacrifice of all the generations that would come beyond the one animal. That makes it a truly costly offering. It is a sacrifice of that genetic strain as well as that individual. In the case or Jesus, everything that was connected with sin was killed when He was as we see in II Corinthians 5:21. no

Note: the sacrifice of Elijah on Carmel was a burnt offering. The people needed to give **ALL** to God. Holding back was the sin of Achan and of Ananias and Sapphira. This forces us to expose everything to God. He can forgive every sin, reward every ministry, fill every need, fellowship with us without restraint, all when we give all to Him.

The sacrifice had to be without defect. In the animal this was physical; in Jesus it was spiritual and moral as well. A defect will keep a sacrifice from being whole and innocent. It has to be whole, of complete integrity, complete. God doesn't take partial payments. He doesn't have plans and send out coupons for paying off your debt over a period of time. It's pay up or else. I don't mean that He's nasty about it, but that you're either with Him or against Him. There's no in between. You have to pick a side and stick with it. That's one of the messages of the book of Revelation.

This aspect of the animal puts it in line with God who is without defect. The victim's blood is applied to the worshipper. For a really good in depth discussion of this see the chapter on sacrificial rationale in Alfred Edersheim's book, <u>The Temple And Its Services</u>. If there is a defect, perfection will not come to the sacrificer.

The sacrifice is to have the virtue which we lack. It is to be complete and innocent before God. Animals do not have a moral sense, so their blood is innocent as they do not sin. Jesus had no fault, as Pilate said. They could find nothing against Him. No charge stuck. This no defect is for us.

It was to be offered at the doorway of the tent of meeting. Jesus had to be crucified in Jerusalem. It was outside the city, but was tantamount to being in the doorway of the temple. The doorway is an access point. Jesus is the access point for us to God.

The tent in Moses' day was where man met God. It's the meeting house of God, not the people. It's not like Duffy's Tavern, an old radio show, where the elite meet to eat. We don't go there to meet anyone but God. He is the one we're going to have fellowship with.

This is in accordance with law. The doorway was where the altar was. A sacrifice can't just be offered anywhere. That's why, once the covenant was inaugurated, the high places were out. You have some times when offerings were made at other places, but those were not a part of the sacerdotal system.

We have to go where God is if He's going to get what we bring Him. I know we can hear Him in Yosemite, but for our regular spiritual life, we need to go where He is stated to be. For us now, that is the assembly based on Jesus' "two or three" word and on Hebrews 10:25.

The sacrifice does real good. The good it does would not come apart from the sacrifice. This is done so that the sacrificer may be accepted before the Lord. They were not in "limbo" in Israel. Acceptance was possible.

Acceptance is God's credence in us, not like a loan "acceptance corporation", although in another sense it is like it, not in that we pay the debt over a period of time, but in that God accepts our debt and lets

Jesus pay it. It is His recognition of us in more than diplomatic terms. It is His making us at home. We are accepted **before the Lord**.

This is:

❖ In His presence
❖ At judgment
❖ In heaven

The sacrifice of Jesus gives us all this, **WHEN** we trust and obey. This is both the most complete protection and relationship possible. We are square in front of God, not off to one side, barely in His peripheral vision. The sacrifice is offered to effect this.

Cause and effect. Those are in place here. What we do does something for us, if we are doing what God wants us to do.

Genesis 3:10
2 January 2016

Man's First After Dinner Speech.

Actually, this is only man's second recorded speech of all time. The smartest thing He did was to speak to God and not be silent. Confession is not good for the soul only. It's good. Period. If you won't confess your sin, you're stuck with it.

Rather than being unaccustomed to this, He should have been very accustomed to it. God has to remind him by calling him. God calls wherever we are. Let God remind you. Don't say, "I know" when you've done nothing about what you know.

There are four points to the talk. (He didn't know the three point sermon approach.)

1.   I heard the sound of you in the garden.
Adam spoke **to** God. He was in communication with Him. He recognized the objective existence of God.

Man didn't have to discover God. God was always there, but man had to learn to call on Him after the garden – Genesis 5:26. That was a step backwards rather than an evolution forward since before that time God had called man, and man didn't need to call on the Lord. But, better to go what seems to be back when you need to.

God made a sound. A spirit made a sound. Long before Jesus made sounds in the manger, God was heard. This is not about what Adam heard, but what God made, testifying to the reality of God. No one needed to be in the forest to hear it.

We sometimes think we're hallucinating about what we see. There is a place where because of the curvature of the road if two cars are following one another it looks as if they are both coming at me side by side. I know that's not what it is, but it can still catch me off guard for a half a second as I see them up the road. On the other hand, we always know when we **hear** something. It may be that we don't know how to interpret what we hear or exactly where it's coming from, but we know we have heard it. Sounds indicate reality.

God was in the garden. He was in Adam's space. Let's put it in bold letters: **God is in our space whether we recognize it or not.** We need get a hold of the concept of the God who is in our world. <u>The God Who Is There</u>: Francis Schaffer wrote a book on it.

The world denies that God exists, and to do that they have to deny that He is anywhere. Adam **knew** that God was there. At least he was honest about God, even if he didn't come out into the open right away about himself. His sin did not blind him to who God is.

The devil tried to shade it differently to Eve. In verse 5 he claimed that after they ate they would be like God. Adam know more than ever before that He was totally distinct from God. He did not get to be like God from eating. He was already like Him in having been created. Nothing could add to that, nor could anything Adam did elevate him to God-status.

Man is not God. That is the beginning of some wisdom right there. Man did not "create" God. The quote about if there was no God man would need to invent Him is unnecessary, but there's no "if" in the equation. We may not be able to prove God to the atheists because He does not fit into their logic shapes, but all those who deny God cannot prove their profession of faith in no God.

2.   I was afraid.

Here's where he starts to get into trouble.

From fear of God he goes to being afraid of God. Fear is respect; being afraid is terror. The two are totally different.

Man was the one who turned the corner. He'd had been better off taking the road not taken. When it comes to obeying the word of God we really know what is the best road. God saying it makes it the best. He would never deceive or lead astray. Revelation is always to our good, even when it shows what will happen to evil. We profit by avoiding the evil.

I would say that being afraid is a whole new category for Adam. I wonder how he even came to invent the word for it. It would be like me inventing a name for an emotion I had never felt before and which I had never heard anyone speak of before. He had lived in a world without terror. No noise in the night made Adam fearful. No animal had caused him anxiety. He didn't fear burglars or vandals or murderers. He didn't succumb to any circumstance. He didn't believe he would run out of anything or not have enough. He didn't have to think about sickness or dying.

I know I'm conjecturing about some of those. Much of my thinking in that regard is colored by C. S. Lewis' novel <u>Perelandra</u> which imaginatively describes a world where man never fell, but I think Lewis had a legitimate point that man could have steered clear of temptation and moved directly into something greater, even if it wasn't what he had pictured in his book.

Man was not by nature as created meant for fear. He was meant to be in constant connection with God. He had his work in the world and his relation to his spouse, but the point of reference over it all was

God. Modern man only has the two - work and relationship, and they're redefining the second one. The complementary nature of the sexes is being abandoned for a psychological synapse which will not bear the weight of man's nature.

We need the three: God -> work -> spousal relationship. They need to stay in the cycle. I'm not saying that this means that everyone has to be married, but in order for marriage to work it has to have these three things which are all a facet of the fulfilment of the mandate to multiply. For the unmarried, and indeed all of us, there are other familial or social relationships which need to be lined up.

3.   Because I was naked.

Now Adam attempts to explain himself. Imagine you are called to the platform and told that the topic of your extemporaneous speech would be: Explain Yourself.

His situation has changed, and he freely admits it. I saw myself without you. That's what Adam has to say now. That's the terror of nakedness. It has nothing to do with body parts being visible. How can we be without God? To see ourselves without Him is to see our imperfections, faults and creaturely nature.

He also saw himself in isolation from the woman and all the rest of creation. He had been alone in a way before, but now he's really alone.

The knight of mirrors destroyed Don Quixote in "Man Of La Mancha" by showing him what he was in the flesh. I've seen two stage versions of this, and they just fill the stage with mirrors to devastate Don Quixote. The knight of mirrors was unrelenting. Don Quixote couldn't depend on his illusions any longer in the face of these repeated revelations.

We need to see, not in the mirror of the world, but in the mirror of our God what we are in the spirit. That's what I Corinthians 13:12 is about. We long to be clothed and thus be in relationship with God as we see in II Corinthians 5:2-4. It is being clothed with Christ (Galatians 3:27) which does it.

Adam had it all and lost it all. In Jesus we can have it all again.

4.   I hid myself.

He withdrew. It is man who does this, not God. We have made concealment our God. We don't want to be seen because then our sin would be known to God and everyone else. So we insist on privacy and closed doors. Privacy is everything you don't have to explain behind the curtain of privacy.

We need to be revealed through Jesus. The road to shame-free existence is in God's provision for our sin.

God fixes us; we don't.

We need to be found like the sheep, coin and son. Our being found depends on God looking for us, as set forth in the cases of the sheep and the coin, and in our return, as set forth in the case of the son. Both elements are part of the picture. God's part, though is many times greater than our part, but without our part we won't get His part.

When someone is coming out of some situation of insensibility we say, "Speak to me." When someone in silent in a conversation we say, "Speak to me." God has given us permission to speak. What will you say to Him?

One more thing. God will find us, but we need to agree to go home with Him. He won't beam us up without our agreement. So, let's be agreeable to God.

Genesis 14:19-20
5 January 2019

What would you like to be known for? Here's someone that the only thing we knew he did was to bless. I think we could safely say that blessing was his game, as they would have put it in far earlier times.

This is the blessing of Melchizedek referred to in Hebrews 7:1.

Verse 19

He = Melchizedek.
Blessed = act.
Him = Abram.

There were two people involved in one act, the one party giving it, the other receiving it, all at the same time.

Melchizedek was the priest of God. We don't know how. He is not part of the Aaronic line, since he predates it by many centuries. He is a genuine priest of God, perhaps the only priest in his generation. No others are mentioned at this time in scripture. He kept a relationship with God even when the rest of the world ignored Him. This alone shows that it is possible for all kinds of unlikely people to be in relationship with God. After all, at this time, Abram himself was such an unlikely person.

Blessing is what Melchizedek does. It is a pronouncement about what God produces. It doesn't control God. It's not "magic". It enrolls God into the life of another. Blessing unleashes God. God will do what He will do, but there are times when we can point Him at it. Who do we want to point God at?

Abram is blessed here in verse 19. God is blessed in verse 20. Everyone in the picture gets or gives a blessing. That in itself would transform any group or church if all they were about would be blessing others.

Blessed be Abram is a direct statement. He said it about him rather than to him. it was truth rather than a commendation designed to swell someone's head or a wish which may or may not occur. Melchizedek knows that God is going to do something with Abram. God is going to do something with every one of us. Even if we don't let Him, He will, but in that case we may not like it.

Abram had just fought a battle to rescue the nephew who had selfished him out of the best land. Abram knew that whatever ground He occupied was good because God was in it, not because it had any particular quality in itself. He hadn't yet "believed God" (15:6), but he had acted in the strength of the Lord.

Abram is blessed, not by circumstances or luck or ability or entitlement or government dole, but by God Most High. So are we.

God Most High is El Elyon transliterated from the Hebrew. Many claimed to be God or were called God, but there is only one God **MOST** **HIGH**. That is the superlative, and it doesn't change with circumstances. No one else ever steps into that role. It is always only the same.

Most High. He has the highest position, the greatest vantage point. He can give the most. This is all true of Him, but Melchizedek makes it even more clear WHO He is.

He is the possessor. People get to be possessors by buying something or being given it. Even then, they only "own" something if they pay the taxes on it, and then they only own it until the next time the taxes are due.

We can't control possessions outright. At best we are caretakers of them. They can be taken away from us by tragedy, legal action, government seizure, etc. Even from a spiritual standpoint we regard this earth as a stewardship situation for us. Not so with what God owns. He is absolute possessor. He owns with no lien against Him. He owns inviolate. Nothing can be or will be taken from Him.

He possesses heaven **and** earth. Man thinks he owns at least earth, and he's got his eye on heaven as he did at Babel, but God owns both. He is the sole proprietor with no partners.

Heaven is God's home, the place where everything is decided, the place from which everything is created. All our descriptions of it, even those in scripture, are probably not adequate. Not because God didn't show it or tell it properly, but because we don't have enough words to share it properly. The most opulent places we have seen will fade in comparison to heaven.

Heaven is total magnificence because it is total God working out His person in the presence of the universe. God possesses this. No one else is on the title deed, nor have they ever been on it nor will they ever be on it nor will they ever be on it until we get to heaven. The earth is only the Lord's, but heaven will be ours, too.

This all means that the earth is owned. It owns nothing, despite the Sierra Club and the National Geographic Society and all the New Age ideas presented to us in popular films and books. The environment is not in charge. We could have 100 ice ages before Jesus comes back, and it wouldn't change anything. I'm not impinging on politics. Politics has impinged on scripture and truth in this regard. They are the trespassers.

God owns it. That is why we care for the earth. It's somebody else's property. We're always more scrupulous (or should be) about the property of others. It's not that we respect the earth for itself. The first real Christian perspective I got on this was from Francis Schaeffer's Pollution And The Death Of Man written almost 50 years ago. He pointed out that the roots of secular environmentalism are pantheism and earth worship. We need God worship.

Abram is blessed because God blesses him. Melchizedek can only pronounce it. God has to do it.

Verse 20

God needs to be blessed by us. He's great without our blessing, but our blessings focus our lives on His life. The value is to us. That's why the need. God doesn't want us to be without.

Blessing is to be our game when it comes to God. We don't bestow good on God, but we say every bit of good we can on Him. This God Most High who blessed Abram is blessed by us. In doing so, we acknowledge His status and position. That's what belief does. It accepts and acknowledges and approves what God has said and done.

Melchizedek knew God. To know me is to love me. That's what many people say, but it's not always true about "me" whoever the "me" might be, but it is always true of God. To know Him is to see His total person. We don't plumb the depths with our intellect, but we recognize all that He is.

He is to be God Most High, not only in external reality, but also in our hearts and mouths. Believe with your heart, confess with your mouth. That is the sum formula for blessing God.

God is blessed for what He has done. He is credited with it. In this case, God delivered Abram's enemies, the four kings, into his hands. It wasn't Abram's generalship or resources which did it, but God. We will have to fight, but it's not as though all depended on us, but because all depends on God. Even when we lose an earthly battle, it depends on God – not the defeat, that is, but us. We depend on God. We continue to look to Him. If we don't, we lose.

That is the message of every battle Israel lost. It was not that God wanted them to lose, but that He wanted them to realize the value and absolute necessity of looking to Him. Carried into exile, they were to look to Him. Here, it's victory. There can be no victory without God in it.

Melchizedek wanted Abram to acknowledge God, so he acknowledges God in his blessing. What we say of God when we bless Him shows what we really think of Him.

I have a long list of enemies – physical, spiritual, personal, technological. God delivers every category into my hand. There's nothing that is beyond Him. He takes care of things in government offices, doctors' offices and everywhere else. He gets what we need to be done done.

A seeming defeat is only a delay, not a defeat because God is with us, and nothing is over when God is in it. It's not the thing, but God. It's not like Frosty's melted self waiting for a North wind to bring him back to life in the Rankin-Bass animated show. Everything can be evaporated and blown to the antipodes or else incorporated into the rings of Saturn or sent to a quasar, and God doesn't bother to go after it. He doesn't concern Himself one iota with what has been lost. He doesn't fix. He replaces with something new that hasn't existed before. It's always better.

Abram gave Melchizedek a tenth. He did this spontaneously, not by legal prescription. There was no pre-battle accord regarding this. He did it from love, not of Melchizedek, but of God. We always show love to God by what we give to others. God never gives us so little that we can't afford to give to someone else. He never gives just enough without any leftovers.

By giving, Abram acknowledged the truth of what He was told. We need to acknowledge the truth of God by our giving. We begin by giving ourselves to Jesus. Then, we turn to what's left. There's nothing that says to the world we believe in a thing more than our giving our money to it.

We love because He first loved. It's the same in the blessing. We need to be blessed by God, and, in turn, we need to bless God.

But, to end with what we need to begin with: how can we be blessed by God? By doing His will and associating with His people.

Deuteronomy 18:15
11 March 2019

Jesus was not a latecomer or an afterthought. He was part of the plan from the very beginning, even before there was a plan. However, not to be negative, but he was a ringer brought in at the right time to replace someone else ------- us.

This is one of the great prophecies of the Old Testament. I'm not sure how many people know it. The apostles knew it, though. It is quoted in Acts 3:22 and 7:37.

Jesus had a space to step into. I can remember feeling at my father's funeral when I was 33 that I was being propelled into a new position in life. Jesus felt none of that. He was where it was always intended that He would be.

Moses was far seeing. He saw beyond his day. He never thought that with him everything came to an end. He knew God was going to continue to speak to His people and that He would eventually do so with one to match the stature of Moses, although He would actually exceed it.

As great as Samuel, Elijah, Elisha, Isaiah and Jeremiah were, they did not come up to the measure of Moses in the overall scheme of things. They were almost all specialists compared to his universal general practice. Isaiah comes the closest, but it is Jesus who fulfills this prophecy.

The Yahweh your Elohim. We always deal with the complete God. He's never partial, always personal.

We are used to historical figures who make history. They caused things to happen. They pushed themselves and their lines forward. Jesus was not such a figure. He did not come in such a style.

History is always man's story. What Jesus did was to change history from being our story to being His story since He has always been history and destiny for His people.

God is the one who raised Him up, not Himself nor the flow of history nor popular acclaim.

God raised Him up by overshadowing a virgin. We don't know how He did that, but it could have been as simple (for Him) as becoming a single cell within her which grew to a child and then to a man. Jesus passed through every stage we pass through, both in physical and psychological development. I don't know how it played out, but he didn't skip over the teen years. He started out in the mail room and ended up in the board room. Yes, He was the prophesied one, but He learned from the things He suffered. (Hebrews 5:8)

Jesus knew our experience and was able to speak to it. He

spoke to the human situation more clearly and plainly and simply than any other prophet.

He came up because God raised Him up.

When I was a young child I once saw one of those theater organs that comes up out of seemingly nowhere to fill the platform. I couldn't have been more than 5 or 6, but I still remember the way my eyes bugged out when the fellow playing the organ and the organ came up out of the stage. This ought to impress us even more.

He is for **you**. God doesn't need a prophet. We need one. The prophet speaks forth the words of God which we wouldn't have if the prophet didn't speak them out to us.

No one could take on being a prophet from his own will. At least that's not how it's ever presented in the scriptures. They had as association of prophets of some kind in Elisha's day known as the sons of the prophets, but I don't know on what basis those so categorized became prophets. I don't know of another era in which such an arrangement was mentioned in the Bible.

The prophet is something of a phenomenon. He was called the seer at one time because He saw things. He saw what others couldn't see. We have the great story of Elisha asking that his servants eyes would be opened to be able to see that those with them were greater than those against them. John on Patmos saw things and gave us certainty about the victory coming to us in the future. God has mysteries which He wants to reveal, and He does so through His prophets, but we have to acknowledge that they are of Him.

We give Him heed. That word, heed, forms the bookends of Revelation in 1:3 and 22:7.

The prophet is not just another public speaker or teacher. He is something more. This one was going to be like Moses. God spoke to Moses Face to face. This prophet would be God speaking to the world.

A prophet brings nothing second hand. It's right from God's mouth. The prophet is a megaphone, making God heard by people who are in danger of ignoring Him.

This one would be like Moses. He would be a person of authority, bringing God's word. He would stand before them for God. Only, in the case of Jesus it would be a step further. Jesus would not only be the promised prophet, but He would also be God standing before them.

He would come from among you. He was going to be an Israelite. Jesus was from Judah. He was one of them, not a foreign advisor. This is why we have the incarnation as we have it. God shows that He takes care of things in-house.

He will be from your countrymen – a second way of saying it, just in case you didn't get it the first time. This emphasizes the fact of the point of origin. Even when they belittled Jesus as being from that nowheresville Nazareth, they had to acknowledge that He was one of them.

The prophet was going to come. This is because they didn't' want to hear God direct as set forth in verse 16. What if they'd been willing at Sinai? Would there have been such a delay of centuries in the sending of Jesus?

The prophet will come. That imposes on them a responsibility. You shall listen to Him. Shall means this is right.

Listen – pay attention to. He who has an ear, let him hear, it says seven times in Revelation 2-3. The burden of listening is on us, not on God. He sent the prophet to tell us. He did His part. The tragedy of the New Testament was that there were those who received Him not.

When you listen to someone, you take in what they say. You get it. Still, they have to make sure you got it. Sergeant Carter shouted, "I can't hear you!" over and over to get the marine recruits in "Gomer Pyle, U. S. M. C." to talk louder all the time. He wasn't really listening. He was just wanting them to speak and to speak what he wanted them to speak. God, through the prophets, is asking us, "Are you listening? Are you getting this?"

You don't have to listen to the news or go to political meetings. You have to listen to God. He can speak in the still small voice. He can speak from the mountain. He can speak beside the sea.

We are to listen, not ignore or let it in one ear and our the other. If God comes, we are to receive Him. That is a principle throughout scripture

They only heard Moses from time to time, and you have to wonder if everyone ever got to hear him all at the same time, given the numbers of the people and the lack of electronic public address systems. We have an opportunity every day to listen to Jesus.

The disciples knew. Now, you know it, too.

Exodus 6:6
23 January 2015

What I need to hear today. When I wrote this down, that's what I thought to myself. So many times we read the scriptures, and we know they're all true and right and that they will give us life and guidance, but this one day, I knew I was getting what I needed that very particular day.

God tells Moses what to say. Moses made up nothing. Revelation is always only from God. It is not ever humanly originated. Both Paul and Peter also made this point.

Therefore,

Because I declared myself on this issue in verse 1,

Because I am the Lord in verse 2,

Because I appeared to Abraham, Isaac and Jacob in verse 3,

Because I established my covenant in verse 4,

Because I heard and remembered in verse 5,

This happens in verse 6.

That's a lot of becauses to the therefore of what God is now going to have Moses tell the children of Israel. It's never just, "Because..." or "Because I said so." It is because He lives and made them and continues to care for them. He is willing to give them what only He has.

This goes to the sons of Israel, that is the whole nation. It's all the covenant people who get this. God is not silent. He now makes four points.

1.   I Am The Lord.

We shouldn't need to be told who is going to do this the second time, after we already had the identification in verse 2, but we get it. I - Me Alone - No Other.

If nothing else, we need to hear this that we are not alone. God is on duty. There is no busy signal. There is no answer machine. There is no unanswered call. No one is standing by. He picks up before we ring.

God doesn't prove Himself. He merely proclaims Himself. This is the personal name of God, not a classification of Him.

He is the starting point of all faith. There can be no faith until God is in the picture. Abraham believed God. He didn't believe statements or truths or facts about God. He believed God.

It is not the covenant which saved, but the act. It has always been believing God and obeying Him.

Why does God always say **the** Yahweh, employing the particular article, when there is only one? This makes the specific even more specific so that we won't miss the specificity of it. This is not a serially occupied office such as that of a president or governor, and the article points that out. It's not a name which many people could have such as George or Jane. Even if someone named their child Yahweh, they would not be Yahweh for it is more than a name.

Yahweh's identification is the ground for all theology, revelation, morality and wisdom. You name it, He's the foundation of it. Even science. We have that in "in the beginning..."

God is the reason. He **is** reason. That's why saying, "There is no God," makes one a fool. What we say always makes a difference. It always counts. So, say what you mean, and make sure what you mean is what really is so.

Saying does not create, but it places us. To say that there is no God is not to disinvent God. It is to place oneself outside the pale of God. We are the ones who do the disconnect, not Him.

To believe God is not to create God. It is to place oneself in His camp.

I am the Yahweh. Look no farther.

2.   I will bring you out from under the burden of the Egyptians.

I will bring you out from under the burdens of the Egyptians. God had made provision for them in Egypt, but He had not endorsed the slavery nor the burdens. God leads us to all kinds of places, but He doesn't guarantee a Paradise in them, only His presence There are other elements in this aeon which can get in.

God could have just beamed them to the promised land, but how could anyone have learned anything from that?

We may bear the burdens imposed by others, but our God bears us.

Who is stronger? The ones who put burdens on us or the One who bears us and our burdens.

The Egyptians used the Israelites for their purposes. God has a better purpose for the people.

We look at the weight of the burden, the object that is bearing down on us. God looks at us. We should look at God. That's the point of this declaration.

The children of Israel so often looked elsewhere.

- ❖ They looked at the Red Sea ahead of them – not at God with them.
- ❖ They looked at the army behind them – not at God who was greater than them.
- ❖ They looked at Moses being unseen – not at God – and then made a "seen" god who was not God, though it was called God.

❖ They looked at the giants in the land - not at God who wanted them to have what the giants had.

Ultimately, we're not talking about where we're getting out of, as though it were a physical location which controlled and limited us, but about getting in Jesus.

We have Jesus to look at. He's better than a brazen serpent which was just a one dose prescription which wasn't renewed and which afterwards lost its potency. He is for eternity.

3.   I Will Deliver You from Their Bondage.

It gets worse. From burden to bondage is a terrible step. They are bound. They can't get away.

Almost everything we are in, we can walk away from. We can tell them to take this job. We can leave a house we don't like. We sometimes have to pay the penalty, such as a deficiency balance, but we are not chained to the land like the medieval serfs were.

Israel was bound. She was an entire nation bound by the most powerful nation of the day. The artifacts that have survived should be enough to convince us of Egyptian power in this situation.

God would deliver. He would get them out of it. It's not just release, and then you're on your own. It not just a brief reprieve. It's not lessen the rigor. It's not gradually getting them out of it.

It is deliver.

On one night.

With gold thrown in.

They would be gotten out. that's what made the later wanting to go back so heinous. When God delivers, you are out. No one has a claim on you. Pharaoh thought he did, but he was mistaken.

To deliver is to take from one place to another. God provided for forty years and then brought them to the promised land.

4.   I Will Redeem You With An Oustretched Arm And Great Judgments.

God will buy back. They always belonged to God, but he's willing to pay to get them out of hock. To redeem is always requires spending something. There is a cost for it. It is to pay money or some kind of currency, whether physical or otherwise, to secure a release. God's power has been exerted on their behalf.

It costs God power. The fact that He is omnipotent doesn't take away from the fact that it costs Him. God is not an effortless being. He always can, but it costs. I don't know how to explain it beyond that, but knowing that God exerts Himself makes it more imperative than ever that we exert ourselves in thanksgiving to Him.

An outstretched arm is an active arm. It's not one folded across his chest or dipping into the popcorn bowl. This is an arm at work.

God is active. This would not have happened on it's own. He was going to do that through the ten plagues and through the deliverance and preservation and conquests to come.

These judgments were not God being nasty. They were judgments on the oppressors of His people. God used what the world would understand to deliver His people. He didn't send Moses to cry or whine or grovel or say, "Pretty Please Pharaoh." Every one of these was a terror.

Pity it took ten. The Egyptian people suffered much for the hardness of Pharaoh. God didn't make him be hard. He only made him stay the course he himself began.

At the time God said this to Moses, none of the people could imagine these. They might have remembered that God had sent some plagues on Egypt probably around 500 years earlier as recorded in Genesis 12:17, but unless they knew something from oral transmission that has not come to us in the written word, we don't know what those were. My guess is that they were nothing like the ten. The living generation of Moses' day had no point of reference or past record to go by. What God was going to do was unprecedented in their lifetime. He was going to interfere in the course of the world. He was going to do this for Israel.

We're not left out of all this. Our yes is coming. God is going to interfere for us. The setbacks Pharaoh created by his refusals to let Israel go did not stop God. He is a saving God and a delivering God and, if need be, a meddling God.

I need to hear this every day.

This is not merely a serving suggestion. It is a serving schematic.

Members are not numbers. I have heard church members referred to as giving units. Sometimes they almost seem more regarded as ball players who belong to the club until they are traded or retired under the complete control of the powers that be in the congregation rather than as Saints directly answerable to Jesus.

We are not statistics even though statistics can be complied about us. Our service makes sense out of the statistics. It also makes sense out of us. We are defined by what we do for God.

Serving or carrying, doing things to or for God - all were accounted for. All were numbered in what they were doing. They were all in place. They were all authorized by the commandment of the Lord. That was one tribe only. This is true of every church member as well, for we are all part of the body.

They were categorized under the two headings of serving or carrying. I don't know if this is the totality of how we could look at it, but much ministry fits under one or the other of these headings.

SERVING:

Service is rendered to a person, not a thing.

They were serving God in the sacrificial system. We don't do that anymore as Jesus did all the sacrificing already, but we serve God in our worship. We serve when we assemble, sing, pray, give, proclaim. Hebrews 13:15, 16 is the great New Testament charter for this concept.

God is the person who has everything. How could you do anything for Him? Because He lets you. It's kind of like Dad letting you do the mower when you are still fascinated with it, but not quite deemed ready for it. God deems us ready the moment we are saved. That's because Jesus has cleansed us and the Spirit is in us. We need to grow in that, but we are truly career ready day one.

We serve God by doing what God wants us to do to others. We are more than middle men. We are part of God's entire team. The sheep of Matthew 25 were the servers not the sayers. They were separated out because they were destined for better things. Service means doing something for someone else. The six categories of the parable are:
1. Food
2. Drink
3. Shelter
4. Clothing

5. Visiting the sick
6. Visiting the prisoners

Service thinks of the other person. It alleviates his needs. Those presented in Matthew 25 are representative, not exhaustive. We're not off the hook if we have all six of those as though no other avenues of service were available, and I'm not sure that Jesus implied that everyone did all of them, just that these were the things that the sheep side was doing.

The early church did a lot of serving at tables. In Acts 6 they took care of the needs of fellow Christians. In Galatians 6 they served the household of faith. We need to say to one another, "Set 'em up," and then start dispensing stuff.

We serve by sharing. The Christian life is a sharing life. Christ shares with us, and we then share in Him with others. No one should have to ask us, "Will You Share?"

By way of comparison, serving focuses on what we do for others; carrying focuses on what we do to others. In either case, it's all about others. Jesus showed that the Christian life was not a self life. It is a First and Greater life. First, get saved yourself. Greater, save others. That comes from the "Greater love has no man that to lay down his life for his friends" speech. Dealing with others is always the greater thing.

CARRYING:

Practically, one way we do this in praying for others. Paul talked about his care for all the churches. Much of that was accomplished in prayer. Jesus carried us in His prayers in places such as John 17. We cannot always literally carry someone, but we can take them to God.

Carrying lightens burdens as we see in Galatians 6:2. It's easier to carry something on the move than to stand and hold it for a long period of time. The movement gets the blood going and keeps our arms well supplied. We do something for someone they can't do for themselves. Open a door for a wheelchair bound person. Take a blind person to a place he cannot see. These are little things, and I've done them, but they are necessary things for those people, nothing extraordinary in a spiritual sense. We are to carry needs, not just pass by as the priest and Levite did on the Jericho road.

In the financial realm we speak of carrying someone. We mean that we don't force them to pay up right away. We give them time to "get it". Patience does that with people in life situations.

We have an incredible sense of "justice". We know what a person should do. When we carry them, we give them time to learn what they should do and to adjust to it and to get to it.

We wouldn't throw someone out of school on their first day

because they couldn't read <u>War And Peace</u> in the original Russian and explain to the least sophisticated class member what Tolstoy's theory of history was. Patience is giving them time to learn.

We carry someone when we are patient to allow them to arrive at where they are going. We wait for them to finish.

We carry someone when we shoulder the responsibility or blame. I don't mean we lie and say we killed Cock Robin when everyone knows full well that Jenny Wren did it. But, we carry the full load. We don't blame-shift like someone says I always do. (I guess I am wrong.)

Ministry in the church is serving or carrying. We serve the word; we carry needs. I guess I see that model in Acts 6.

Personally, I'm a word server by either spiritual engiftment or natural psychology. I'm not really tuned to human physical needs like I am to scripture. That doesn't mean I don't ever do things for others, but that's not where my main strength lies. I think it's wrong to categorize as "so heavenly minded, no earthly good". The prophets were called to be heavenly minded. The church is called to be both, but not every individual is called to be both.

Serving focuses on the person. It can be God or other Saints. It focuses on meeting them and connecting with them.

Carrying focuses on things. The carriers in Numbers 3 and 4 carried the parts of the tabernacle. They carried them and also assembled and disassembled them on the road.

God lets us do things for Him. He could have spoken the tabernacle from place to place, but by carrying it, the Levites learned. The learned about the things of God and their meaning and their position in the building. They learned what it kept to keep the covenant going.

There's no superiority in one or the other between serving and carrying. The apostles were not superior to the deacons. The practical people are not superior to the eggheads. The point is that everyone is numbered and accounted for as a servant of God. All are connected to Him by what they do and are.

No matter who gets our service or work, it's God we're working for.

Exodus 16:6-7
26 January 2013

I can remember liquidation sales being advertised when I was a kid with these words always prominently featured in the ad: "Everything Must Go". Then there was the song where fellow who lost his girl to another fellow was saying to her about the new one, "He'll Have To Go". I don't know that people bought out the store or that the jilted fellow got his girl back, but when God says something has to go, it has to go.

Verse 6

So – in this manner, at this time.

Moses and Aaron form a unit. There were times when they were separated, but here they act in concert. Even more, they were in concert with Yahweh. Any time you team up with Him, you have an unbeatable combination.

We see here the value of unity in ministry.

They were facing an angry mob. The pitchforks and torches were out. These were Thumbs Down Dissatisfied Customers. We have the same in the church. Congregational and ministerial solidarity tends to come apart at such times. I'm not saying we should swallow anything anyone says and go along with it like the father and son taking their donkey to market in Aesop's famous fable, but that, no matter who comes out against us, we need to look to God rather than man.

Anger alienates those in ministry from one another, but it shouldn't. It should bind them together. Moses and Aaron expressed themselves together. There was no contradiction in them, no, "But this..." to what the other said. No pointing to one another as to who should be the target of the people's rage.

"All" was the key. They addressed the group. We need to act and operate as a whole. Special interest groups in the church fracture and splinter. See I Corinthians on this.

They all had to sign on to this. No one could make a separate peace.

There are times when we need to break away, especially if it is from the world, but in the church, we need to find a way to circle the wagons to be unified.

The sons of Israel had a common ancestor: Israel. They had a common brotherhood in that they were all sons. They had a character. From Romans 9:6 we know that descent alone was not the defining element to being a son of Israel. You have to do what Abraham, Isaac and Jacob did before you.

They were a group whether they wanted to be or not. It's the same with the church. We are sons of God – Matthew 5:9. We cannot choose our brothers. We are a unit. We are connected. We don't decide to be. We come that way when we come into Jesus.

Evening was, for them, the beginning of the day. Genesis 1 always talked about the evening and the morning were the first or second, etc., day. God starts the day working for them. He gets up when we go to sleep. He provides all the time. This is not only one enchanted evening

What came at evening? Meat. See verse 12. God provided for them apart from their possessions. He went outside what they already had to give to them. Our possessions are not our source or resource. God is.

They didn't kill their livestock, and they couldn't grow food on the road or shop at the nearest Edom-Mart or Moab-Mart. The animals that they had were for sacrifices to God or to form the start of herds once they settled down rather than for them right then on the road.

This may be the truth of the century: God provides for us apart from our possessions. In accounting terms, we need to list God at the head of our assets. He will tip every balance sheet in our favor.

You will know this, by experience, not merely by intuition or by being informed by another. To know is to have this information fixed inside.

This is about the Lord. Yahweh. He uses the covenant name even before the covenant is established. The I Am that spoke to Moses from the burning bush is this same Lord. We reiterate Moses when we say, "Jesus is Lord."

He brought us out. It's over. It's finished. This was not a process, but a single decisive event. God never "evolves" anything, but does it. There was no gradual deliverance. In one night it was done. At the Red Sea it was done in one night. Almost all the battles were one day events. If they weren't, the fault was with the sin of the people as in the case of Achan's sin causing trouble with the conquest of Ai.

Moving on. The cross was one day. Pentecost was one day. Peter's deliverance in Acts 12 was one night, not a lot of legal maneuverings and discovery and motions and rulings and ORAPs (orders to appear), etc. Even long years of gridlock will not stop God.

They were brought out of the land of Egypt. They'd been there for 430 years!

It's hard to move. Inertia will keep you in place. Suction will hold you on the bottom. These people were rooted in place by their history. As a nation they'd had more history in Egypt than in the promised land of Canaan, yet Canaan was their home. Who says you can't go home again?

God can move. Egypt was bondage, idolatry, lack of worship. God **always** wants to get His people out of these things.

Verse 7

Now we move on to the morning. God's work is not exhausted by the night. He has more for the next day. We start to work then, but God has already finished before we even get up. We just get the benefits of His time on the clock for us.

What did they get? Bread. He would tell them that again in verse 12 even though He'd already told them. They were going to know in the night, but in the morning they would see. It would be unmistakable.

Sometimes we see something we can't interpret. They would know what it was they were going to see.

This would be the glory of the Lord. It wouldn't be the sunrise, but the fame of God. This fame was made greater by the provision of the manna. What earthly ruler could provide on such a scale and do so for 40 years away from any natural resources! The manna was a total miracle, an "only God" thing.

We come to reasoning now. This is a strange reason for showing the glory of God. We would keep our "glory" under wraps for such a reason. We wouldn't want people to know that we are listening to their complaining and getting glory out of it.

He hears. Listening is an attribute of the true living God. Idols were spoken to, but nothing was heard from them. God takes it all in. Only a person could do that.

We hear only what we like, if we can help it. I don't tune in to a rap station. I heard Vivaldi this morning.

God hears everything, even what He doesn't like. He not only hears, but listens. He never tries to tune us out. He wants to hear that repentance from His worst enemies, and He couldn't hear it if He shut them out. We couldn't do that. Some things we might hear would just tear us apart.

What did God hear here? Grumbling. Not enough! We're going to die! We'd have been better off back there! We'd be better dead.

God hears all this, but it's not just grumbling against their lot. It's against the Lord. Against the I AM!

I wish things were different at times. I wish Jesus would come back today (every day). But, being against God, against Yahweh, against Jesus, against the Holy Spirit? No. I can't even imagine the possibility of being against God.

We don't like people to be against us. When they are, we then become against them. Not so God. Oh, He does punish sin, but when they are His people, He holds on unless they actually repudiate Him. Just another thing that only God could do.

We have an addendum in "and what are we – Moses and Aaron – that you grumble against us." When people can't reach God, they will turn on His leaders. It's never a case of the leaders being the target. They just happen to be in the line of fire.

Moses does have a valid complaint, but he follows the lead of God. He continues to lead and work for the people despite their grumbling.

Your grumbling won't move God. He works on in spite of it. It won't change God; He is eternal. It won't discourage God; He brings His purposes to their end. I won't make things better; only God can do that. It won't accomplish anything.

Usually when we're done grumbling we don't feel any better. Sometimes, it is a catharsis, but it changes nothing.

Grumbling cements our hearts to the wrongs or lacks we perceive. That's why it's got to stop. We're not to be partnering with grief. What should we do instead? Pray. (James 5:13)

Yes, we have needs, lacks, troubles, injustices, but our grumbling will not even touch those. God will, but He won't pass through grumbling to get to our solution. Grumbling keeps Him at bay. That's why grumbling has got to go.

God acts when He shouldn't be expected to act. He even acts for us when we have been against Him.

In conclusion, the question isn't, "Why doesn't God do something?" It's "Why don't **you** (or I) do something? Why don't you pray or praise or even let God be angry for you?"

Give it to Him. Whatever it is, give it to Him.

Exodus 33:12-17
10 October 2019 - 16 October 2019

A Leader's Prayer

They have designated a certain time as Pastor Appreciation Month. We don't need for people to appreciate leaders and then go on their merry way.

One of the meanings for the word appreciate is to estimate rightly, and that's what we want to do here. We need for every Christian to become a leader himself. Everyone in the church is to do something for God. That seems beyond so many of us, but then I think of the words of Arvin Moden. In personality, he's a low key speaker, but when he said this it was totally dynamic. He said that if God gives you a ministry beyond what you can handle, don't worry. That's because He wants you to depend on Him to accomplish it. That word resonated with me the moment I heard it.

Don't think when you read this passage that Moses needed that, but I don't. It's recorded for our benefit, also. What Moses prayed is a part of how we will be able to get that help from God. You can appreciate yourself, in the sense of rightly thinking about yourself, better after you have prayed for yourself. Actually, that's true about everything.

Leaders don't come by it naturally despite what is often thought. They don't do it without having to consult with anyone. Even Jesus consulted freely with the Father during His earthly ministry. He was a Son in the house, taking the illustration of Hebrews 3 into account. How much more a servant in the house such as Moses. And if Moses needed this, what about us? I don't know of any Christian leader who is responsible for both the physical and spiritual welfare of millions of people, but Moses shows that none of us can get on without prayer and guidance and blessing from the Lord. Moses had nothing as a person that you don't have.

Verse 12

Moses had experienced great glory in speaking with God personally as no other of his generation did, but that wasn't enough. He had been told to lead the people, but knowing God was not enough by itself. He needed help from God.

People can think that if they just know God, that's all that's necessary. People can know their boss and know what he wants them to do, but they might still be deficient in knowing how to do it and who to involve in what parts of it. Knowing will never excuse from not doing.

Moses gets real bold with God here. God expects His prophets to be bold with the people, but He can take people being bold with Him without getting upset.

Moses spoke directly to God by name. We have that same privilege through Jesus Christ. There's no doubt as to who was being addressed. Prayer should always be that way. It is always to be specific. It's not that God will throw anyone into the lion's den who doesn't pray to Him as happened to Daniel in Darius' reign, but that He won't hear the prayer, which is something far worse than facing a herd of hungry lions.

He starts with almost a, **"See here."** I've added the here part, but he is calling God to account. He is trying to get an answer from Him. What could be more bold and audacious than that. We don't always get details from God, but when it's about something we are to do ourselves, we should ask for them if they aren't given up front.

It all began with what God commissioned Moses to do. It's pretty plain from the book of Exodus that if it had depended on Moses, there would have been no leading of the children of Egypt by Moses. He killed a man and then ran away. He was content with his new family and with his own sheep. (How many times have we felt that what we had was enough when God wanted to give us something more? Maybe, we'll never know.) He made excuses when God told him to go. God had to provide him with evidences and a spokesman. Finally, he went.

God had told him to bring up the people. God's intention is always to bring people up. It is never to leave them down, no matter how they got down, whether it was from their own sin or from the oppression of others.

God, also, involves us in doing His work. He could do it all, but then we'd learn nothing. Teachers always learn more when the teach a subject than they did when they studied it in college. Moses is learning to communicate with God on the job, but for some reason, he expects help. His question is, who's going to go up with me?

Maybe he got the idea from Aaron going with him before that God was always going to send someone with him. Two by two is a pattern that they used in coming into the ark, and Jesus used it in sending the disciples out on a preaching tour. There are times, though, when God sends people out alone, particularly among the prophets.

Moses does acknowledge two things as coming from God. God said He knew his name, and that he, Moses, had found favor in God's sight. Those are two things that we need.

Many years ago I wrote a song called, "My Name Is Known" about the intercession of Jesus in heaven for me before the Father. The idea that God knows my name through Jesus is a striking one. At this time in Moses' day it was only told to Moses that God knew his name, but I believe he knew them all. That knowledge of God is the base on which we can rest securely. We're not wandering around out of our minds now knowing who we are or having to "find" ourselves as people used to do. We are known completely and exhaustively by the one who made us and who loves us. No one can go out and minister in the name of the Lord if he is not known by the Lord. That was one of the sad features of the parable of the five foolish virgins who were told by the lord of the feast that he did not know them. We don't have to suffer such a tragedy.

God knows Moses, and Moses found favor in His sight. We're not talking about a disposition, but a gift. Favor should be seen as grace. God took Moses, even though Moses was a headstrong murderer who went away into the wilderness to hide out from the law and from the world in general, and called him to work for Him. When God wants to use us in His work, that is one of the greatest favors He could bestow upon us. It means that He trusts us to do something for Him, that He wants us to do it more than anyone else.

Every Christian has a ministry. Not just the preacher in the pulpit or the elder or the Sunday School teacher. Everyone is a leader because everyone has someone following after him. Everyone has a ministry, and it works for us because God knows us and because we have found favor in His sight. We know that because God has given us grace through Jesus which is even more than what Moses got.

Verse 13

Moses expresses his prayer. He doesn't think it, saying to himself that God knows everything. Yes, God knows the heart, and the Spirit, in our covenant, can groan for us with groanings too deep for words, but we need to express ourselves first. He only steps in when we can't get it out right enough.

What Moses has already gotten is as a result of what God has done. God always gives first, but then we pray. That's how it is with prayer. Real persons are involved and real results take place in the real world. There's nothing ephemeral about it. You don't pay your money and take your chance – you pray your prayer and get your answer.

I don't know why he said, "if", about what God had already expressed Himself on. It could be humility or saying that since you have done this, I'm asking that. It could be a sort of help my unbelief mode. Sometimes in scripture, though, what in English is expressed as if, really has the force of since. The point here is that we are at the key factor. Even if Moses is conjecturing in an if, He is doing so about God, and we may conjecture more surely and securely about Him than we can about

66

anyone else. All of His requests are rooted in the person and revelation of God.

Moses asks one multi-part request for himself and one single request for the people. Those in leadership need more from God so that they don't ever depend on themselves for wisdom or resources. Even though there were times when Moses missed the boat, he knew enough when he was praying to God direct to get the ducks in the right order.

Show me your ways. I once heard Mike Adkins (of "A Man Called Norman" fame) preach. It was one of the best messages I've ever heard. Over and over, no matter what the circumstance or problem involved in our lives, he said that our prayer should be, "Lord, teach me your ways." So simple, yet so basic and so advanced all at the same time. It covers everything.

We know the world's ways. We think we know our own ways. But, in none of these cases do we know where those ways will really end up. When God reveals to us His way, even if we only know it a step at a time, and even if we don't know ahead where we'll land, we know that it is His way and that it will take us along the right route in the right manner to the right destination.

God's ways are there for anyone. Even the sinner could find them if he would repent and call on the Lord to show Him the ways. They're not on our maps, though, and there are no road signs along the way to designate them. We now find many of them in the scriptures, but a lot of times we are in the same situation that Moses was in. We need guidance for something that is not written out. Being shown is always better than being told because that means that the one showing us is with us when we go the way.

Further, Moses turns the tables. This is so He can know God and find favor. The world asserts that there is no God or if there is one that He is unknowable because they do not believe in revelation. Revelation, of course, is the real key to everything that we know about God. There is so much we would never be able to deduce if we weren't told. Science thinks it can penetrate all the answers if given enough time, but with the increase in knowledge and computers and technologies I don't think we're any nearer to a final full complete answer than we were in the days of Hippocrates or Pythagoras. We may know more than we used to about some things, but we don't know everything about anything.

Spiritually, we need to be shown the ways of God. we need to get them from God alone and have no one in between. I know I said we are leading others, but what we are leading them to do is to follow God for themselves.

When we see the ways of God we will not only know what is

right from what is wrong, but that we will also know the right way to do things and not merely do them our way. God would spell a lot of that out to Moses in the book of Leviticus and other things revealed to Him, but He doesn't ever show everything. I don't think it's because He's stingy, but possibly we couldn't understand it all any more than a two day old baby could understand an algebra book written in Arabic or because we need to stay dependent on Him rather than thinking we can just roar off on our own.

I think the second request is more along the lines of keeping favor rather than initially locating it or else it could be because favor is such an amazing concept that Moses really goes strong on it. Maybe he keeps repeating the favor business because it is so unusual and beyond the norm, and because he needs to convince himself of it.

The favor is connected with God. It is in your sight, as Moses addresses things to God. The last verse talked about how God looks at us, but maybe we need to ask ourselves the question, how do we want God to look at us. God so loved the world, but He didn't save those who didn't receive Jesus. Both truths have to be in place as set forth in the Gospel of John. God doesn't look at us with X-Ray eyes that undress our Spirits, but with a disposition to see us as His and to do good for us. Favor means that God sees what He wants to see, not because we put it there, but because we believed and repented and came to Him.

For others, Moses asks that God would consider the nation His people. What Moses is asking is for God to take ownership, to have pride in them, to maintain them, to look out for them. He knew that the people were God's nation, but still he asks. It's so easy to quit being God's nation by getting into sin. Such a request will help the nation to stay on the way.

Moses sees beyond the few people he works with out to all the hundreds and hundreds of thousands on the march with him. We, too, need to see those who are marching to heaven with us and be concerned about them and their continuing relationship to God.

Verse 14

God replied. He always does one way or another. We may not know the answer the moment it's given, but we will know it. Usually, we say it could be yes or no, with a possible addendum to the yes as being later or to the no as being turned to a yes based on repentance.

In this case, God gave two answers. Two are better than one, but, then, anything that comes from God is better than anything that does not. In speaking of presence and rest we might think in terms of the pillar of cloud and fire which showed God leading them and the rest as the promised land they entered into. It's even greater for us as

Christians because our rest is in heaven where God is.

My presence will go with you. We don't have to wait for heaven for that. God gives assurance. Some people think it's wimpy to pray that God will be with people, yet I find that promise given many times in the Bible, particularly in the end of the book of Revelation.

God's presence is something that is real and that is known. I don't mean we put on special glasses like they did at some of those old trick movies where creatures weren't revealed on the screen without the glasses. I don't know the optics involved in that, but I do know that there was a trick to it. There's no trick to this. God shows up with His people when they turn to Him and ask Him to be there.

The second thing God's people get is rest, and it is given to them by God, not by the government or by the health or tourist industries. Rest is more than having the bell ring for quitting time. It is having all the effects of toil and work removed and having new resources in our spirits and bodies so that we can face what is next. The New Testament tells us that we definitely have it in Jesus in Hebrews 4:9-10.

Now, I don't always like that. I like it when the ducks get in a row and stay in a row, but even if they want to, the world and the devil don't want them to, and they will often stir things up. Sometimes, it's just nature that does it through some kind of weather or natural event. Storms don't know about our plans.

What we need from God is not taking away the negative, but putting in the positive. God could take all that away, and when we get to heaven that will be part of what happens when God wipes away every tear from our eyes. Right now, we need for God to take a hand and give us what we need and cannot get for ourselves or from anyone else.

Verse 15

Moses says that if the presence is not with us, don't carry us there. The presence is indispensable. Without it, we should dispense with the going.

Sometimes people are sent to places that their leaders themselves won't go to, such as when a general sends units of soldiers out to battle. It started out with the king being at the head of the army as with King David in the Bible or King Arthur in legend, but eventually, the king stayed behind the lines and the generals under him did, too, so that it was only the warriors who were out on the battlefield.

There are some places we don't want to go. There are cities in the United States that I would not choose to walk in alone at night. There are routes I wouldn't always take in my own area, not because of people, but because of bad roads or too many deer out at night creating a hazard. (People who have not lived where deer are liable to pop out anywhere along the country road won't understand that, but after living in such an area for over 20 years and losing two cars to deer which jumped into them, it is a great concern to me when I'm out and about.) I don't want to go to where there is danger or a potential of loss. Moses didn't, either.

This is sort of similar to lead us not into temptation prayer. God wouldn't lead to the wrong place anyway, but we are seeking assurance for ourselves in such a request, and God is not beyond answering what we need. The only thing He won't answer is a prayer that is not made.

Moses is basing his request on all these things being the reality he must live with. When God is not with us, anything can happen, but when He is there we have a protector at our head or at our side. We always base our requests on the reality of God and His presence and His grace.

God can clear the road for us and give us a safe landing in a narrow place. We should really take the approach that if God won't go with us, we don't want to go there.

Verse 16

Then, Moses gets practical. He asks the how question. People can sometimes get into trouble asking God, "How?" He doesn't always intend to tell, so we need to make sure that our question is not designed to force God to open up to us or to put us in the driver's seat once we understand how it can happen so that we think we can do it ourselves. In this case, Moses, like Gideon after him, was asking for some re-assurance. He already had the assurance in the word of God, but some things from God are so great, that we have to make sure we heard Him right.

How will we know we've found favor? It's one thing to tell someone that they've found favor with you, but what is the concrete way that they will know that they have found it?

Many times the question is almost more important than the answer. It's a matter of framing it the right way so that you get the real answer. You can ask in the wrong words and get an answer that fits those words rather than what you really want. For the Christian, this is where the Holy Spirit's groanings too deep for words work, but Moses, despite his high place in the nation and with God, didn't have that.

We need to identify with whoever God has put behind us. It's not just Moses alone that is involved in this favor issue, but Moses and the people. A good leader identifies with his own people. It's never, me and them, but always the single word, we. That is an all inclusive word which has no limit or boundary. Any number of people can fit in it. Moses was dealing in the millions.

He's guessing now, but he's doing it based on what's been revealed to him. Is it that God takes His people places that He doesn't take anyone else? Actually, God does do that. He never led any other group of people to a promised land. He doesn't take any but the Saints to heaven.

This is a real place. It's not Never Never Land. That's what the tour guides on the Story Book Canal Boats in Disneyland told us when we went by the little place where they put the boats at night. They said, "That's never never land, because we never take you there." We went on that ride numerous times during the 30 years we lived in California, and they were right. They never took us there.

God will take us somewhere. He'll get us where we need to be and where we'll receive a blessing. It's us who will get this. God's people are distinguished from all the other people on the earth. It's not just that we're a little different, but that we're all the way different. That's what it means to be holy. We are holy because God makes us holy, not because we earn it or work up to it. That's why the name, Saint, applies to every Christian. God is the one who sanctifies or sets apart. No one does that to himself. If God doesn't do it, they don't become.

Verse 17

God answers Moses in Moses' terms which were really God's terms to begin with. He does not speak to us in riddles as the "oracles" of the Greeks did. The most famous one is when they said to Croesus that is he went to war with the Persians a great empire will fall. They failed to tell Croesus that it would be his empire which would fall, not the Persians'. God is not ambiguous.

God will do what Moses has spoken. That is one reason why we pray, so that we can get what we ask for. I don't mean that God always gives it as He does answer in the negative at times, but that we have no assurance of a specific answer without a specific request. If you want God to do what you have spoken, you first need to have spoken.

It's like going to a restaurant. I don't know about you, but even if it's the kind of place I like, I don't think I'd ever just say, "Bring me whatever you want," to the waiter or waitress. I scrutinize the menu to pick out exactly the meal I feel like having on that day. Sometimes, even then, they bring the wrong thing. I ordered one item to go at a fast food place the other day, and when I got to where I was going to eat it, found that they had given me a different one. The different one was all right, and it wasn't worth going back, so I ate it, but it wasn't what I had ordered. God gets it right.

When God gives us what we ask it's because of His favor and knowledge. We asked, but the answer is totally dependent on Him. We

71

could ask for something at a restaurant that they didn't have, and we wouldn't get it. We can ask God for anything because there is nothing he doesn't have.

The bottom line of all this is that God wants to do something with us, and He knows us. I'm not inviting people to the results of my activities when I teach or preach.

This is not just true of the big shots, but of every Saint. This prayer is not for the preacher. It's for you because your life is a sermon to everyone around you, and God can help you make it a great one.

We have knowledge of us by God, favor from God, God's presence, rest, God's action. Anyone can lead with that behind them.

Exodus 14:14
26 January 2019

Battle Truth. This is what's true during the battle. It's contrary to our normal mode of operation, though. We expect to do something in the battle to win the battle, to get the triumph.

Before the battle, we need to pray. After the battle, we need to give thanks or praise. During, though, we need to shut up!

Back seat driving probably causes more accidents than it provides safety. After all, who could tell God? (Romans 11:34-35)

Moses is telling this about the Lord because the Lord has revealed it to him in verses 2-4 above.

The Lord will fight. He will be active about what the world is doing.

We are inspired by slogans about fighting. Thus, we pumped our soldiers up with the film series "Why We Fight" by Frank Capra. An old commercial said over and over again, "I'd rather fight than switch." (I'd rather fight than use their product, but then I wasn't on television, so I didn't get to say that.) In our American history we argued with Britain using the slogan "Fifty-Four Forty or Fight". I don't think it actually did come to a fight. We settled for the 49th parallel and went on. Still, the focus was on fighting. It's always assumed that under the circumstances, whatever they are at the moment, we will fight.

I'm not sure that everyone who saw Capra's films, for example, wanted to fight, although seeing them for the first time almost 60 years after they were made, I can see the sense they try to make. It's not that we want to fight, but that we can't just let these things go on without doing something about them. We don't fight because we are persuaded, but because we must. The enemy is attacking, and we're in the army.

God fights alone in this instance. He did not use any human agency, and there doesn't seem to be any angelic involvement.

God fights. He exerts Himself against Pharaoh, the most powerful ruler in his day. He engages in battle. He grapples with our enemy.

We may be in bondage. We may be in total physical subjugations. We may not be able to move our little finger. We have a God who fights.

You wouldn't think you'd seen a John Wayne movie without a fight somewhere. He was known for fighting and winning. Even John Ford's tribute to Old Ireland, "The Quiet Man", has a real battle at the climax showing just how unquiet the quiet man can be. It's like Wayne has to fight. As long as we are in this world, God has to fight for us even more.

You wouldn't know God was at work in the world if He wasn't fighting the world. God is fighting for you.

We can fight for our country, our principles, our way of life or truth, justice and the American Way. Ultimately, though, all fighting is for someone, not for itself.

I can remember a Lulu cartoon when I was a kid. I don't know why, but this one has stuck in my head. Butch and some other kid are having a fist fight on a viaduct of some kind. Lulu gets under it, saying, "I always wanted to have two boys fighting over me."

God doesn't fight over us; He fights for us. He fights in our place so we don't have to. He fights to bring us good, doing it so we can get the good of it.

We shop for someone. We bake a cake for someone. We make a meal for someone. They don't have to do it, but they get the benefit out of it because we did it for them. The children of Israel didn't have to fight Pharaoh. That would have exhausted them and may have led back to bondage. They got the benefit of being free to go their way uninhibited.

The "while" part of the verse is a sort of "Meanwhile Back At The Ranch" moment showing what we do while God is active.

We'd like to help. We'd like to cheer. We'd like to get in on the action. We are to keep silent.

God is to do it all. He is to get all the credit. We are to restrain ourselves. It's hard to know when to do that, but if something is beyond you or what you can organize, and you have prayed, that is the time to rest rather than fight and work. After the battle there will be things to do.

We Americans have the "I've got to do something about this" attitude. We have a hard time leaving it alone and expecting it toe come home wagging its tale behind it.

People can wait so long, and then they have to do something. Or so they think. That led to problems for Abraham with regard to Hagar and Saul in regard to everything.

Faith means we let God do it all. We don't help. He is the great life guard. Unlike earthly life guards, He won't drown if we struggle, but we might as He will let us go our way if we insist on it.

Silence means we don't tell God how to do it. We don't try to redo His wisdom or improve on it. We don't try for any credit in the matter when it's all over, either.

If you're gonna do it, do it. That's what Jim Hamill would say about crowds that started with a sort of weak applause. We need to go the other direction. If we're going to be silent and let God do it, then let's do it. Instead of swelling the sound, we need to turn the dial all the way down to Zero.

When we get out of the way, we give God room to act so He can deck the enemy and keep him from even injuring us in the slightest degree. We are always safe from friendly fire when He attacks because He has pinpoint accuracy which could flick a single angel off a pin point on which thousands were dancing.

This is not the silence of quietism which does nothing, but the silence of faith which has spoken its piece and is now waiting on God to do the piece faith has spoken.

Note: in the next verse God told them what to do. God did the fighting so they could go forward.

We are not forgotten. They were not to fight, but to move to God's ground for them.

Exodus 4:22
22 January 2018

God always has a plan beyond the moment.

This is out of the burning bush. God speaks when no one thought He would say anything to them. They had been in bondage for centuries and seemed stuck there. We can have to wait five minutes for something we don't want to wait for and it seems like an eternity. I once went to a ceremony that was so long that I later told someone I was telling about it that I was still really there. They really were there.

God was coaching Moses. He knew he was going to need it as, even if he had been trained in public speaking in his upbringing in the education system of Egypt, he wouldn't have been doing any such official public speaking in the last 40 years.

We feel stuck in our moments. We have a bad job. There is a horrible family situation. There is an illness or medical condition that is not getting better, but constantly getting worse. Finances are running away, and what's happening at the capital is going to be the end of us. They were stuck in their moment, but God is greater than any moment.

We are not alone in our moment. God comes to us in the moment. He always has a plan beyond the next step. In this case it's about what to do after Moses does the wonders and Pharaoh hardens his heart.

The wonders are the credentials. For some reason, even though God made everything, He is not believed on the basis of His word alone. These are the things Moses did. The staff/snake untrick and the leprous hand alone should have done it. They were really beyond man. Take the next nine and you've really got something.

The Egyptians did tricks, but Moses could do the real thing. People are still fascinated by all this. I don't think they broadcast "The Ten Commandments" anymore every year like they used to, but Nielsen ratings showed that the viewership always rose sharply when the plagues part started. People knew and tuned in because that was something impressive.

God would harden Pharaoh's heart, but it was after Pharaoh hardened it himself. Pharaoh set the course and God made Him stay on the path.

This wasn't just for Moses as though none of the rest of us were to be in on it. it was for us even down to this day. God gives support to His people through what He has Moses say to Pharaoh. God gave him his lines long before he needed them. At that time Pharaoh was going to say to Moses that he wouldn't see him again, but Moses is going to have the last word. I'd have been tempted to say to God, "Why can't we just

start here with the killing of the firstborn and get the whole thing over?" For one thing, I think God wanted to show that Pharaoh had time to repent. Why didn't he? This also shows that Pharaoh deserved to get the plagues he got.

One thing we can give Moses. He didn't try to shortcut the plan. He went through the entire program as God set it out. He had problems later such as breaking the tablets or striking the rock, but here he did as he was told.

Moses is going to say this. He is not to be silent. He is not to be intimidated. He is not to leave Pharaoh in the dark.

God didn't say that Pharaoh would listen, but that Moses should say.

The preface to it all is, "Thus says the Lord." We are to speak God's words not ours when we speak for God. We are not to guide people by what we think, but by what God says. The whole of scripture is, "Thus says the Lord." it's all the communications of God.

Even what man or others say is revealed by God through His word for what it is. The serpent said, "Has God said..." Moses says, "Thus says the Lord." There is no asking or wondering or speculating. God is not on Twitter. This is what God says. Thus, it always has a particular content.

Israel was Jacob's name given after he had wrestled with God, so to speak. When we pray, we are still grappling with God, not with the thing we are against. It's not that we're against God, but that we're engaged with Him, and there is always going to be a back and forth nature to our experience both in the world and with God. God recognizes us as a legitimate offspring.

Israel is my son. A father always has special concern for his own children that he doesn't have for everyone else. It's not that God is mean to the nations, but that He looks out for His son.

Israel had gone from being one man to seventy people to being a nation. 430 years will do a lot to any group of people. They did not disintegrate in either prosperity or slavery. They only got greater.

They were a total unit. They kept to their blood. Israel was characterized by its grappling with God. It didn't let down. We know this because they continued to pray.

People are protective of their sons. They were Yahweh's son, I Am's son. The creator, infinite/personal God was the one they were the son of.

Son recognizes relationship. Israel is not like a son. Israel is God's son.

God is the Father, the point of origin. The son is in the direct line to inherit from the Father. The son is given all that the Father has.

The son is not free at this time, but the Father is just about to set the son free.

The Father is a deliverer. He frees from bondage. He provides a living as he did in the cases of the manna, quall, water from rocks, etc. He provided a home, the Promised Land. He has an inheritance to give.

The son acknowledges the Father. He's not subservient, but He acts for the Father. Like Richard Conte in "House Of Strangers", he takes on the Father's reproach and bears it, although in this case any reproach against God was man-originated and not deserved in any measure.

Israel is not just a son. He is THE SON. What God would say of Jesus, He says of Israel here. He is my firstborn. He says this of us before He says it of Jesus. This is the one who gets twice as much as all the other sons. He is the acknowledged carrier of the family name. He is pre-eminent. Great things are expected of this one.

Israel didn't push Jesus aside, but was in this position by God's word. When Jesus came, Israel could only stay in that position by getting into Jesus.

God chose Abraham and Isaac and Jacob and everyone in Jacob's line through the twelve sons. Together they constituted the first born. No one tribe or person did. In the church it's the same way. Together we constitute the church. No one congregation or person does.

God confronts the world on our behalf. He stands up for us.

The point of it all is this:

God acts because this is so.

We act because this is so.

Being a son is the foundation of everything. We have a direct relationship with God. We do what we can do because we are who we are.

Exodus 34:9
2 February 2019

ASK BIG

Moses is praying while he is worshipping (verse 8). What a great combination.

Moses was talking to God. Talking to God is the best thing we can do. Adam was in great shape as long as he did that. Once he left God out of the loop, he got into trouble. We need to bring God into everything we are doing. He is really around all the time, but it is our prerogative to exclude Him, but when we do, it is also our responsibility to pay for everything He is not a part of. That's something to think about.

There are really four things going on here in this verse.
1. He has a condition. His condition is really God's condition for him.
2. He speaks to God – and gives his request.
3. He knows the people he's praying about, and he knows that God knows them to the core.
4. He asks God to do something almost beyond belief.

Now to take them one at a time.

1.   The condition he is speaking from is if he has now found favor in God's sight. They've really messed up. we don't usually push our case in that circumstance. Moses, though, seeks something from God, not because of how it is with himself and the people, but because of how it is with God.

We need to stress Moses' understanding that this is a condition he has to be in in order to get anything from God. It's also a condition that can only be created by God, never by Moses or anyone else.

He doesn't plead merit or accomplishment. He doesn't plead family background or other connections. He doesn't plead self at all. It is God's favor which is pleaded. Favor is God's disposition toward us. it is based, not on us, but on Him.

Favor comes to those who have not earned it. Grace isn't grace if you deserve it. Paul plumbs that idea to its depths. If Moses had earned this, he wouldn't have to ask for it. He'd already have it.

A key question before I come to prayer of any kind or any

depth is, what are things like right now between God and me? It can't be, what did they used to be like or what are they going to be like, but what are they like now? God hasn't changed. We ask this because it gets us lined up with Him. it orients us toward Him. There wasn't any magic in Jerusalem, but when Daniel prayed in that direction He was orienting Himself toward God and not toward anything in Persia.

There are times in which the terms favor and grace seem to be used interchangeably. We know about grace from the New Testament. It's almost the keynote word other than the name of Jesus, but what about the Old Testament? What was its status there? The word grace doesn't appear until Ezra 9:8, still I don't think I'm out of line to introduce the word, grace, into the discussion here. Favor showed up a lot before then, but grace appears to be a step beyond. Grace carries out favor to its ultimate logical conclusion. Favor seems to be more specific, but grace just keeps going. It covers everything, especially as it is presented to us in the person of Jesus Christ. God is preparing us for more. There is always more with Him.

If God gives grace, He'll give everything. It's hard to comprehend a person who can give everything - health, wealth, livelihood, healing, a home, a hope, transportation - you name it, God is in the business of giving it. In a way, I think the general in the film "Babette's Feast" had it right when he concluded that even the things we have rejected are given to us by God. I think he's standing on some solid ground because everything is given to us by God, and His grace is so great that it can go beyond our refusal.

God sees us. We know that. In this case He sees us through His own disposition, not through our actions. That is what saves us.

I think that Moses assumes that God is looking on him with favor, but he shows his humility by that word, "if". This is not a doubt, but a confession of lack of self merit in the matter. It shows that this is God's act, not ours. We can never take God for granted on the basis of our own conclusions and situation, but we can always take Him on the basis of His own word, and can speak to Him on that basis without wondering if we're doing all right to do that or not.

2.   He speaks to God and gives his request. We wouldn't like it if someone called us up and all we heard was, "Hello. Hello. Hello." We'd especially not like it if they said nothing specific after we said, "I'm here; what would you like?" So many times that's how our church services are. we go through the motions without treating God as if He were really there.

There was a time in history when people might not have known if they had God's attention or not, but coming through Jesus Christ, as the Christian does, it can be known absolutely that we have God's attention. That name is what gets it, both in terms of our making the request in it and in terms of our being in Jesus positionally.

By the way, when he says, "O Lord," here he's really saying, "O Lord." He's not saying, "O Yahweh." This is Adonai, the Hebrew word for Lord, describing God's position, not a euphemism for His name.

Lord means owner, ruler, boss. How many people are readily willing to acknowledge God as boss? That's what the world is fighting right at this very moment. **IF** they abort at will because it's their body, choose their own gender despite their genetic make-up, don't have to follow scripture in discerning who is a Christian and who is not and even how one gets to be one, to give a few examples, **THEY** are boss. The question then comes, of course, who can be boss over anyone else? If, for example, they exert their right to be boss in choosing their gender, that right doesn't include in it a right to boss to reject anyone else's assessment of the system. It doesn't change the chemistry, either. They are only, in such a situation, licensed to lead themselves. If they are licensed over anyone else, then everyone can be licensed over them. It has to be fair, after all, since that's another one of their big bugaboos. They reject both God and man, but they do it by licensing themselves, not apart from others, but over others.

Only God is licensed over all. He is the owner, the Lord, so He can do more with our requests than we can. That's why this is so much more than a suggestion box. Why do we need to make suggestions? Not so He will know, but so that we will know that what we get could come from no other place. This cause and effect relationship puts coincidence all the way out of court.

The request is to let the Lord go with His people. It's not to **be** with us, but to **go** with us. This implies that we are to be going somewhere.

We go all kinds of places. God can go with us to any of them or through any of them or get us out of any of them. It's not whether you want Him or not. He goes. When God goes with us, we are not alone. This is Moses' request. The pillar of cloud and fire hadn't left them. We see them still there in 33:9, e.g. We shouldn't want God to go along ahead of us where we can get out of His sight and do a little something on our own. We want Him in our midst because whatever we are in, we need Him there right at the time we need Him. He can see and guide and advise and work for us there, and there's no doubt **He's** the one doing it.

In a way it almost seems that if we are going to ask God to do anything at all, this is something we are going to almost have to ask Him to do. If He can't go with us, either maybe we shouldn't go there or we won't be able to do anything there.

3.   He speaks rather bluntly about the people he's making a request for. He doesn't try to make them out to be o.k. when they are not. He lays it on think about how bad they are. In order for God to act, He has to do it all, because there's nothing they can do for themselves. They are obstinate and have iniquity and sin.

A person could be obstinate for the good. They could refuse to be moved by the devil or the world. That, though, seems to be more along the lines of being steadfast than being obstinate. The connotational foundation of obstinate is that it stems from something inside the obstinate person. They are not standing firm on a purpose or principle, but they are refusing to move. They are being obstructionists. They won't go, but they won't let anyone else go, either.

The older translation calls them "stiffnecked". It's the idea that they are not flexible. They cannot turn and focus their attention where God wants it to be. They can only look in the direction their own body looks, and then they can only go where they are looking. They set their own course. There is no way for them to see anything outside the field of their own person to correct their course or show a worthy ultimate destiny.

They were a stiffnecked people. We are told not to do stereotyping or profiling, yet in this case, it was true because God had a right to declare it so. The whole nation as a whole was this way. Only two would prove not to be so – Caleb and Joshua – but their day wouldn't come for a while yet. In this case the generalization fit the nation by and large, but it did not fit without exception every individual in the nation. I'm not saying it's all right to brand or label, but that sometimes groups are what they are labeled. If they are wearing the wrong label, they need to repent and change their contents and get a better label which will do them some good.

Moses didn't make this assessment out of the blue, though. He does it after the episode of the golden calf in which all Israel from Aaron down seems to have participated. I would question if Joshua and Caleb were in on it, but if they were, it makes the story even better for they repented and saw the error of their way while the window of repentance was open. After the calf, if the nation had gone God's way, I believe they would have gone right into the promised land without doing all that zigzag wandering about in the desert.

4.   Now, we come to the unthinkable. This could not even be imagined if it wasn't for God. The request begun earlier is continued here. It's not enough for God to be in their midst if they are no good. They have to get their sin and iniquity out of the picture. It cannot be erased by simply saying, "Sorry." Time doesn't erase it from the memory of God. Time doesn't turn sin into boyish pranks to be laughed over in

later life over port and cigars down at the club. There is only one way that sin can be dealt with, and that is for it to be pardoned, and only God can do the pardoning.

A pardon doesn't mean that you didn't do the sin. On the contrary, it states by the nature of it that you did it. What it does is to remove the penalty from you. It doesn't make you good, nor does it remove the guilt so that no one could possibly think you had ever done anything wrong. It doesn't deal with your record, but with your person. What it does is to make it so that you are no longer accountable for what you have done. It's not the offence that is pardoned, but you are pardoned. You are excused not from the assessment of what you did, but from the consequences of it. there is nothing between you and God. Everything has been set back to the original specs.

That is a major event. Every act is done, not just to the person it is done to, but to God. It's not that someone has cheated his neighbor when he has perpetrated a fraud, but that he has cheated God. Just as everything good done in the parable of the sheep and the goats to the least of these is done to Jesus, so everything bad done to anyone is done to God. The entire universe is connected to Him. He is imminent over creation, but connected to it in every way.

I wouldn't believe any of this would be possible if Jesus hadn't said it was, and if He hadn't told us that He had done it. Who could look at the entire history of humanity up to the point of Jesus and predict that someone would come along who could and would say to anyone, "Your sins are forgiven," as Jesus said on more than one occasion showing that this was not an isolated unique event, but something that Jesus intended to do and keep on doing.

But it gets bigger and better than forgiveness. The request is that God would take the people for His own inheritance.

God provides His own inheritance. He doesn't need to take one from anyone else. He doesn't need to be given anything. He has it all, but the request is to take the people for His inheritance, that He would bring them as close to Himself as \he could.

The inheritance was not merely something that was passed on to someone after you, but it was regarded as the entire estate which formed an entity, a whole. The inheritance was the wealth of the person who had it.

Moses was asking God to make us into His wealth. I got a chill over my whole body when I wrote that last sentence. It is like something beyond reality, yet we know from the New Testament that it is reality. We, the people who were created and who sinned have been redeemed by the blood of the Lamb and made into a kingdom and priests and are now reigning on the earth.

That's not all of it, however. It's a two way street. We are God's inheritance, but at the same time He gives us an inheritance which makes everything that Howard Hughes left seem like a poverty pittance. God gives us His Holy Spirit. He gives us Eternal Life. He gives us a place beside Him in heaven. He is in our midst there. What more could anyone give anyone?

If you learn nothing else from this verse, learn this thing. Whatever you ask of God, ask BIG. You cannot ask beyond what He has for you.

Exodus 24:10
23 March 2019 – 2 April 2019

We usually want to see before we act, but here we see the proper order when it comes to getting to God. Go with this flow, and you'll arrive.

Being united.

Being on task.

Seeing God.

Those are the three things this verse is about. Actually, the first two are prerequisites which are in place in the preceding verse, but I want to talk about them here because I don't think we could get to the third one without them. That doesn't mean that if you get up a club with your neighbors and work hard, you'll see God, but that seeing God is not something that happens for any individual alone in isolation from the rest of life as the old mystics had it nor is it something that comes out of the blue to people who are not walking God's way. God can do anything, even reach out to people without their working or being united with others, but those two things raise the likelihood of seeing God if that is what you want to do.

Americans are pretty much used to the idea that they can go wherever they want and see whatever they want. The airlines and tourist agencies would give one to think that if human ability could get you there, you could go there. There are even people who have booked passage on the first commercial flight to the moon, although that hasn't yet been offered. We know that there are places which are either too dangerous to go to or which are prohibited by our own government at time. I won't argue one way or another about whether anyone should be able to go to those. Probably most of the time the restrictions are correct, but if I was a hero out of a Clive Cussler adventure novel, I'd just go anyway and let the government thank me afterwards. Here, though, they were going to get to see something that they wouldn't have seen any other way.

Even Moses didn't get to see God by himself. He was told that he could see the back of God in Exodus 33:19-23. In this present case it could be that they weren't going to see God close up so it wasn't life threatening like a face to face encounter would have been or that they weren't going to get to see the glory, but only the person from a distance in a generalized sort of way. I may not be able to explain the difference between this account and that one, but I don't think God was being inconsistent.

The players on the field here, from what we read in the preceding verse are Moses, Aaron, Nadab, Abihu and 70 elders. The 70 are not here because they are the elite rulers of the people who get to do things the people don't get to do, but because they are representing all the people on this occasion. There's no one person seeing something he can't get others to believe he saw. 74 people saw this. That's a big solid number.

This is a matter of faith which begins, not in what we believe about God, but in how we act together. I don't mean to imply that unity alone establishes truth, but that we're not going to be the only ones going to heaven, and we might as well learn to cooperate now while we're here.

We need to be united. Jesus spent a lot of time in talking to the disciples about unity in his talks recorded in John 13 to 17. Unity was espoused by God long before that. The twelve tribes were to be united with one another and with God. To do that they had to never be united with the nations surrounding them.

Unity is always an exclusive arrangement. It connects us with some people and disconnects us with others. The trick is to get the connection right to begin with. Once you know that, anything else that comes along claiming to be a part of it can be safely rejected because you already know the truth. I'm not talking about living in a rut, but about living in the truth. Culture and patterns change. If Paul and Silas were transported into a modern worship service, I wonder what they would make of our music, for example, whether it be the "old" hymns or the new praise and worship stuff. I don't imagine that even our oldest pieces would satisfy them emotionally. There's nothing wrong with changing in those areas, but at the same time there is also no mandate that change must occur. If it does then the praise and worship people are going to find that their normalcy is not normalcy at all, which is the case in reality.

Anyway, we're not talking about a consensus style gathering together based on styles of worship or beliefs, but about being united to God and Jesus completely. They got that by being circumcised and being included in the covenant. We get it by clothing ourselves with Christ and by subsequently having Him in us, the hope of glory.

It's not a "You and Me, Jesus" world. We do walk with Him, but walking with Him brings us into contact with others with whom we will walk. The consequent unity of being united with other members of the family makes all of us stronger. No one is lessened or weakened. If they are, then the unity is not being handled the right way. There are no second class Christians or below in the kingdom. All are on a par in being linked with Son in the same way as everyone else and to the same extent as everyone else.

Lincoln thought the world would little note his comments at Gettysburg. How wrong he was. When we are united, the world will take note. That's because real lasting unity is such a freakish occurrence in this world. People may not come to Jesus immediately, but they admire such connection in others. Eventually, the hope is that they will want it for themselves, especially as we reach out and invite them into it. Outsiders in the Old Testament days didn't have an invitation, but now everyone does. We are not merely inviting them to join us or come to our location, but to see God. The pure in heart get to do that, and when we are cleansed in the blood of the lamb, that's us.

We need to be on task. A lot of people are committed to doing their job. If things come up to get them off track, they'll say, "Just let me do my job."

Jesus talked about occupying until He comes. He gave us the parable of the talents, the parable of the minae, and the parable of the servant left in charge who abused his charge. The point of all of those things is that we are to be on task.

Now, I can't reach into a file and bring out a folder detailing everything you are to do. I'm not sure that it's like that, anyway. What it is like is someone who sees someone they admire doing great things, and then they want to do such great things themselves.

We all have our own ministries and gifts. Unity is disrupted when someone fails to recognize that and comes along and says, for example, that you can't be a real Christian if you're not witnessing or baptizing folks or praying so many hours a day or reading the Bible so much a week or - well, you can supply the thoughts of others that have been heaped on you. That is a Pharisaical type approach of putting a burden on someone instead of helping them.

I can't get specific, but you can when you pray and search and seek. Sometimes you never get a specific mission statement for yourself, but the best thing you can do is to be known for knowing Jesus. The disciples did that, and when you do it, you'll be doing something they did.

In striving for unity with others and ministry for ourselves, we are walking in the way.

Three times I have seen an eagle flying in the air. Once was a few years ago on the Saturday before the 4th of July. A few days later on the 4th itself my wife and I saw one (possibly the same one since it was in the same vicinity) flying across the road. Then a couple of weeks ago I saw another one flying. (Since the time of the original entry I've had a couple of further sightings.) I'm not saying that I can guarantee that you can see an eagle if you drive down the roads I went down, but I am saying that I wouldn't have seen them if I had just stayed home and not been out in the world.

God isn't hidden away in some inaccessible place as in a treasure hunting adventure movie. He is there wherever we are, but we will be more likely to see Him if we're going places. In this case the two places I'm talking about going are unity and ministry.

So. Seeing God. What does that entail?

We don't see a physical being. God is Spirit. To see Him, then, is not to see something with the physical eyes. In many ways, just as they did in the wilderness, we see the effects of God in the world more than we see God in Himself. We see His power at work in the world. Wherever we are we need to erect, rather than a "Men At Work" sign, a "God At Work" sign because He is at work everywhere.

The first place we see God is in our hearts. This is not to imply that He is not real or is a figment of our imagination, but we see Him inwardly long before we'll ever see Him outwardly. We see Him in our salvation, our freedom from sin and guilt, our renewal. We see Him in the presence of the Holy Spirit inside us. We see Him in the changes the Spirit brings about inside us. Yes, people can develop themselves and master themselves in certain areas, but only the Holy Spirit can change anyone from what they were to what they should be. We just let Him, and we cooperate and do what He says to do when He says to do it.

We see God in our own situation. We all have trials and crises and heartaches and lacks. Being a Christian doesn't lessen those. It doesn't reduce them or take them away, but what it does do is to give us the strength to keep on. We also see answers to prayers of things that we need coming to us in no other way than through the Lord.

We see God in others. He's not in us alone. A God who could only fit inside me and in no one else would be little more than a genie at best or an influence at least. We see God when we recognize what He is doing in other people's lives.

Then, we get to see Him in a place where they could not have seen Him in the old covenant. We see Him in the church. The old covenant was a nation covenant. It was at best a sort of old boy net with no provision for any social or spiritual mobility. In the church, all kinds of people get in on things and have a part in them.

Finally, although not exhaustively, we will see Him Face to face in heaven. I don't know what we'll see. They could paint a picture of Harvey in the famous comedy by that name, but no one can paint a picture of God. We just have no idea of what we're going to see. I don't think it's because God is keeping things from us, but because it is so far beyond what we could even comprehend that it would make a cubist painting plain as day by comparison.

What is the benefit of that? We will see Him as He is (I John 3:2). We see that God is really God. There will be no doubts as to what we'll see. We'll see the face, the identifiable features of God. We'll know it's Him when we see Him. Seeing Him, we'll know who we are like never before. We enter into life more fully than we have done so before. Seeing God is really the far, far better thing.

He is the God of Israel. Their own God, not somebody else's. We are now a part of Israel which is the totality of the people of God. He is our God, not someone else's. He's not an inaccessible power, but a person with whom we can communicate.

This verse gives a very unique fact about the situation of God. They saw a sapphire colored pavement under His feet. Now, God doesn't have literal feet, and He doesn't need pavement to get around (I found out that I need pavement last week when I almost careened down a country dirt road with only enough room for one car at a time and no shoulder to get off to safety), but He walks there because He wants to walk with us. He doesn't float about at will, but takes our paths for His paths. His paths are not common dirt, but beautiful stones and metals. Everything about heaven is beautiful.

I have seen many internationally known personalities in my lifetime, but I never got to associate with any one of them, even for a snack, much less live with them. I am going to live with God. I am going to be in fellowship with Him forever. Those people saw where I am going. It's real. It's fact, not fiction. But for now, I will unite and work. The seeing is sure to come, and whenever se see God, we always want to see more. Whenever we see more we will be satisfied, but we'll still want more because there always is more.

Two last things. People will promise to come see you, but when time goes on, you begin to doubt. I was supposed to see a famous Christian singer three different times. He never came. I don't doubt that he exists, but I'm not sure I wouldn't doubt his coming if he were announced at a particular time. Presence removes doubt. That's why Jesus came, and why He is coming again. We have to hold on to faith.

Next, we may wonder what God gets out of all this? I remember when our first child was born. When she was a baby I would look at her and think that someday she'd be able to talk and we could carry on a conversation. I was not disappointed by her talking. God isn't by ours.

Exodus 33:19
2 February 2013

This is God's response. It's like one of the judges at the Olympic figure skating. Each one holds up a number (or they used to). Ten is the highest, I think. Here ten is God's favor. It is not an assessment of our actions or character or merit or intrinsic worth, but of God's favor. Grace is always a 10. It is never anything else. It is never a fraction. It is never partial. It is never inferior. It is never less than God's absolute best. It cannot be any of those "never" things and ever be grace.

In our last episode the children of Israel had made the golden calf, Moses had lost his temper and broken the tablets, and God said He was going to punish their sins. It doesn't look good. they're tied to the train track, and the hero is seven counties over having an ice cream sundae.

After all that, Moses reminds God that He has known them by name and given them favor. (verse 12) So, God says, "I'll lead you."

Moses says (having seen the ten plagues the pillar of cloud and fire, and the giving of the ten commandments), "Show me your glory." As if there was more glory to be shown than judgment provision and covenant provisions. Instead of answer Moses' question, He gives this answer of verse 19.

The answers of God always come in the context of our lives. They are not like random "fortunes" found by breaking open a cookie.

A.   I Myself will make all my goodness pass before you.

God does this personally. He doesn't send an angel to do what is God's job. He will cause this to happen. It's guaranteed.

It is all God's goodness. Who can calculate that?

What constitutes the goodness of God? Not what He does. C. S. Lewis pointed out that it's easy for God to make nice things. It's not who He is. Being the creator doesn't exhaust His person. It's not what He is. He is love and light. He is 100% of both of these.

Goodness is shown in extending mercy to the guilty. We might not feel the least bit of mercy for a heinous murderer. About the only one I do feel it for is Richard Hauptmann, the man executed for the Lindbergh kidnapping, but that's because I have a doubt as to his guilt. If I knew, there would probably be no mercy. There certainly isn't any for Manson, Lacey, Speck, Dahmer. I just can't find it in me on my own, although I do wish that in every case somehow each one had given his life to Jesus before he died.

God shows mercy to the guilty. He demonstrates it; He doesn't just talk about it. God will show that He is good and that nothing we can do will shake that. Compare II Timothy 2:13.

God showed goodness by giving the law again in the next chapter and by leading Joshua and Caleb along with the second generation into the Promised Land.

B.   I will proclaim the Name of the Lord before you.

This is public. It's proclaimed out where everyone can hear it. We don't have many venues where that happens in real space. Most of it is now done in broadcast space or cyberspace, but He was going to do this where actual ears would hear the actual words.

God will continue to be their God. He will not give up on them. There were a lot of preliminary judgments then, and God will send to hell those who don't believe or repent, but until judgment He will not give up working to the end of redeeming everyone.

God lets them have His name, Yahweh. This includes all that He is. it is before them like a picture on the wall adorning their homes. It is before them by advancing and leading them. the people of the world knew the people of the Lord by the name of their God. Moses actually appealed to God on that basis.

The name is before us to be worshipped. It is before us to shield us. It is before us so that we will know God personally.

C.   And...

Up to that point it was what God would do to them. Now we come to permanent principles of God's relationship to man.

...I will be gracious to whom I will be gracious.

First, nothing is said here or elsewhere about God arbitrarily damning anyone apart from anything they did. It is all on the grace side. That's because the sinning which earned the condemnation had already been done and the guilt already assessed.

God decides to be gracious.

People decide to be damned.

God should have destroyed the people out of hand. He would do that with Dathan and Abiram in Numbers 16, but He preserved the nation, even though not all of the individuals in it would make it to the Promised Land.

Nothing in man requires God to be gracious. He chose Israel and stuck by His choice. He now chooses Christians and will stick by His choice. Those of Israel were born into the choice by their parent's marriages and physical relationships. We are born into the choice by our belief and baptism.

Gracious is a character quality. It is to have a giving nature. It is to live without calculation, to give without restraint, to give to the point of bankruptcy (though never to the point or robbing others or depriving them of their property), to give to the undeserving because you are a great giver.

God is really God, the Greater Than Anyone, not just God the Great. He excels every person, place and thing.

God chooses to be gracious. He grants repentance. Through the Holy Spirit we know that God has chosen us. No one can exclude someone God has drawn His circle around.

D.   And will show compassion on whom I will show compassion.

We don't have to say, "Show me." God is a demonstrating God. I can remember the vacuum cleaner demonstrations at Sears in Portland. They continually were throwing the same junk on the floor and then sucking it up over and over. God, on the other hand, does something different every time.

Compassion is not merely a feeling, but a feeling which does something. Pity stays inside. Compassion, mercy and grace always have to do something.   Compassion starts with the heart and ends with the hand. If you don't do something about what you feel, you're not being compassionate.

God always does this on people. We are benefited by God's feelings.

God knew they did wrong by the calf, but He still felt for them. We say, "He made his bed; now, let him lie in it." God wants to re-make our bed.

Up until the judgment, there is no word of God which is final, but His love. Plumb the depths of God, and you **will** find His love.

Genesis 11:6
4 January 2014

This is the power of man which God must deal with. Man is not helpless and weak. When it comes to sin, he can be too strong.

Man is free in will, otherwise God wouldn't need to deal with him. The doctrine of man breaks on the reality of God. Man was made in the image of God to be in the character of God.

The Lord said. He spoke after He saw in verse 5. God doesn't act precipitately. He does wait for us at times, though, to see what we're going to do. He can help us, but He lets us follow our own bent if we don't ask Him.

PRINCIPLE ONE FOR THE DAY: Ask God.

What do we lose out on by not asking? The answer. The right answer.

The Lord said, "Behold." Who is He speaking to? He does He want to behold what? Is it Jesus, the Holy Spirit, the world at large? I think that He wants to bring the attention of everything and everyone there is on us. We are His primary example of what He has done in the universe. God remarks at what we do. Are we giving Him something worthy of remarking?

This says as much about us as it does about God.

They were building a tower to get to heaven, to make a name for themselves, to stay cohesive. Those are the purposes stated in verse 4. Building programs can often be unifiers. Although they can open the door to a lot of differences and politicking as well.

We want what they wanted: heaven, a name, cohesion. There is nothing wrong with wanting what they wanted, but the method of achieving it was all wrong. We cannot get these things through physical efforts or while there is any pride operating at all. Everything that is physical is going to burn.

We can only get these things through Jesus. They could have had them through seeking Yahweh.

What we do is remarked by heaven. So, we need to think it through or better yet ask about it before we do anything like you're supposed to call the utility company before you dig to have them map out underground wires so you don't cut them or dig them up.

They are one people. They had achieved cohesion. That goal had been accomplished. It's not that we cannot reach these goals. It's not that we're to do nothing. But these goals were really the wrong goals for they were attained on the wrong basis. Unity is not a value by itself. It has to be the right unity on the right foundation brought about by the right means. This was a self-produced unity.

Apparently, unity is not a "natural". That's why government throws us when it mandates unity before unity is achieved.

How were they united? Through the same language. This tells us that language is God created, not evolutionary. Communication is a basic. Adam had it from the first. However, we can even have the same language and be divided as Shaw pointed out when he said that the British and American people were divided by a common language.

A husband and wife can speak English at odds. I have known of people who married someone who didn't' speak their same language, but you wonder how that happened, and you know that there can be no lasting marriage without communication.

Language is only the starting point. In this case it led to a common point of view. God gave them the language, but they used it to promote themselves. Do we ever misuse God's gifts which should be used for Him for ourselves? No need to answer that.

This is what they have begun to do. they've made a start. Nothing we do is unnoticed by God. he not only knows what we do, but its status as well.

The tower is a symbol. Literally they couldn't get to heaven by it, but they might have thought that. God didn't let it prosper though, not because it was capable of reaching Him, but because it was a way of controlling the world, and God is in control of the world, not man.

Interestingly, Science Fiction author, Arthur C. Clarke, dealt with towers as the key to world and interstellar development in his novel Fountains Of Paradise. His towers were short cuts to outer space. Their tower was intended to be a short cut to heaven, one which would have bypassed God and put them in the driver's seat according to their thinking.

Nothing will be impossible for them if they do this. Succeed at one thing, and you'll want to succeed at another. If God let them succeed here, they'd keep it up. Thus, nothing would be impossible.

We live in an age where again everyone thinks everything is possible. Only money holds us back, in the current view. (That's why we need more taxes and higher prices.) They even pay homage to that view in the conspiracy theories such as the one in which the drug companies have a cure for cancer which they are keeping from the world in order to make more money off their drug sales. We see it in the energy efficient cars which the auto makers buy up and destroy, not even allowing someone to build one who wants to because they control the patents. They figure nothing is impossible, so they have to stop it to keep it from becoming a possibility.

God is concerned about man's purpose. We are here for God's purpose!!! While this may be shadowy or unrecognized on this earth, in heaven it will all be plain. That's one of the things that the book of Revelation shows.

The irony is that while not everything man purposes is possible, with God's purposes in action – all is possible. See Luke 18:27.

Why would anyone choose a system of impossibility over a possible one? On the other hand, God sees that man can force things to happen or can, in denial, declare that his possibility has been achieved even when it hasn't. This is what must be stopped.

Man must not be allowed to think that he is autonomous. (The concept of the autonomous man came to me from C. S. Lewis' The Abolition Of Man and Francis Schaeffer's work.) We are not our own value system.

THAT'S PRINCIPLE #2 OF THE DAY.

Our true measure is the measure of our God. If we have no God, we have no measure. If we are our own God, we have no measure. God wants to spare us from hell which is where we'll end up if we start from the point of our own purposes.

What resulted from this point?
1. God's confusion of the language – verse 7.
2. Their scattering – verse 8.
3. The name of Babel or confusion – verse 9.

All their purposes and features of verse 4 were thwarted by the remarking of God.

Are there things that God still needs to thwart to bring to a greater place in His purpose?

The purpose of God came to the forefront again in the next chapter when out of all the divisions of man set forth in verse 10-30 God chose one man as the beginning of His movement to unite all men in His son.

Brokenness is not a goal in itself as it was in the 70s in some elements of super-spiritual Christian culture, but it can at times be a road to wholeness. If we follow God to begin with, we won't need to be broken. The sad thing is that between Noah and Abraham there doesn't appear to have been a single man God could have built on.

Why Abraham? I don't know. Noah found grace in the eyes of the Lord. Abraham, I don't know what he found in the eyes of the Lord. But, I do know how I can find grace in the eyes of the Lord. Jesus and Jesus alone. No other foundation but Jesus!

With regard to our nature, God made man as a mover and a shaker. It just needs to be the right moving and shaking.

Genesis 50:25
20 January 2018

This is what Hebrews 11:22 refers to.

How is that people knew they were about to die and made these kinds of dramatic statements? It may not have been just before the last breath, but close in terms of days or weeks.

Joseph has been on top for about 80 years or more. He could have commanded. He could have even had Egyptian soldiers force them to carry out his will. Like Jack Hawkins in the old film, "Land Of The Pharaohs", who had everyone connected with the Pharaoh buried alive with him in the pyramid, they would have obeyed him.

He makes them swear. He does require it. He does get them to do it.

These are the sons of Israel. who knows how many of the other 11 are around? Probably this is all the descendants including his own grand and great grandchildren. The entire nation was in on this. There was solidarity to them. They were all in on it.

To swear is to take an oath, to bind themselves to a course of action.

What did Joseph want the brothers to do? What did he make them swear? It doesn't seem to be anything before verse 22 as that seems a separate incident. It must be that when God does what He promised, they would take His bones. I said "must" which may not be absolutely necessary, but that's what makes sense of all of this. The oath, while taken by these present, would have had to have been kept by their descendents for many generations since they were probably in Egypt about 350 years more after Joseph's time.

It is not wrong to swear. There are wrong methods of swearing, such as those condemned by Jesus in which people use the oath as a cloak of "truth" to whitewash what was really a lie. The very distinction of binding and non-binding oaths totally destroys the nature of oaths. They are all binding if they are anything. There are none that, once taken, you can get out of.

An oath is more than a promise. If I promised to bring you $20.00 next Saturday, and I died tomorrow, you'd get no $20.00. But, if I'm here, because I swore the $20.00 will reach you eventually, even if it doesn't make it on Saturday. In the Old Testament vows were on a free will basis before taken, but once taken, they were inviolate. That's the oath. When they swore they were binding themselves. No one else was doing it to them.

Swearing is always specific. There are certain words involved. Thomas More, the lead character in "A Man For All Seasons", realized that. He also realized that he could not swear to some things.

Before you swear, you have to decide that you are going to be willing to do whatever you swear. Sometimes it's just to believe something, but even that is a doing.

This is Joseph's saying. It is first a declaration of what God will do, and it is secondly a declaration of what Joseph is asking the brothers to do. By swearing, they are believing the first and saying second. This is faith and works coming together here.

God will surely take care of you. They'd been in the land for about three generations now. The famine crisis was surely long over. Their brother was in charge, so he could have released them if there was anything in the Egyptian government binding them. Why didn't they go back? I don't know. God prophesied that they would be there. Did they get too comfortable being in the best of the land, being related to the second in command? Did they just plain get so wrapped up in where they were that they forgot where they should be? God prophesied that they would be there, but that didn't mean that He made anything happen to them. The Pharaohs were pretty capable of doing that on their own.

1.   The point they needed to come to was not where they were, but what God was going to do for them.

We must be convinced of God and His acts. That is our faith. God is the one who is going to do this. Joseph will be gone from the scene, but God will do this. He will never be gone from the scene.

Surely – that word tells us it's guaranteed, absolutely. There's no doubt about it.

He will take care of you. That doesn't mean God is obligated to give them certain "stuff", but that He will take care of **them**. They will be in His care.

We sometimes have more concern over our stuff than over our selves. When I wrote the initial entry it was during a week when I was totally consumed over a cell phone issue.

God is concerned about our stuff. He can give us better stuff and more, like the time He told Judah to dismiss the mercenary army and not worry about the loss of the money spent on them.

When God looks out for me, I don't have to be concerned about my "stuff" – including my own body.

To take care is to look out for, provide for, sustain. This is not a minimal caretaker kind of activity, but TOTAL care. We are to believe this of God.

2.   Once we have the first thing settled, we can do all things through Him who strengthens us.

Joseph was going to be embalmed and put in a coffin for around

350 years. To set that time period in perspective, George Washington hasn't been dead yet for 350 years. If we were waiting for something of that length, we still have way over 100 years to go.

Somehow, they kept track of Joseph's body. Even Cecil B. DeMille did. He showed them carrying Joseph's bones out in his second film version of "The Ten Commandments" (I don't remember seeing it in the first, but then I've not seen that one as much). It's not explained, but I knew what the mummy was they were carrying away with them. When the time came to go in a hurry, they had Joseph ready to go.

You shall do this. Not them, particularly, but the nation, the descendents.

God will - absolute - already done.

You shall - imperative - to be done at the time of this utterance.

Carry my bones from here. The family plot was at the Oaks of Mamre in the Cave of Macpelah. (See 50:13 and earlier in Genesis 23.)

I don't have a sense of continuity with a piece of land like that, although my maternal grandparents were both shipped from Oregon to a family plot in Nebraska. My consciousness of my spirit going to be with Jesus makes a difference.

The point was that Joseph was sojourning in Egypt, but he was not destined for Egypt. He was destined for the Promised Land. So are we, although it is a different Promised Land. Our spirits will go there. God has promised through Jesus.

We can have a choice as to whether we are going there. Let's do it. Let's go there.

Leviticus 10:3
9 February 2013
9 February 2019

This seems cold. It's about the nature of the universe, though. You ignore the law of gravity at the top of a cliff, you will find yourself a pile of goo at the bottom of it.

When judgment comes, it is from man's acts, not God's will. Even the pagans had some glimmering of that concept. Take for example their story of Pandora. She brought all the evils into the world, not the "gods".

The execution of judgment is from God. The responsibility for the judgment is from man. that's why capital punishment in itself, if it is for an actual crime and not for a miscarriage of justice, is not wrong.

Moses had to explain it to Aaron. Aaron apparently didn't know how to understand it. The people of verse two were consumed. Think Jurassic Park. A chomp and a gulp. It was over for them.

People will say, "But they didn't have a chance!" The chance came before they acted. If you fall on the ice, you don't have a chance. I know. I experienced it first hand. Your only chance of not falling on ice is to stay off the ice.

Moses was the sayer of this because Moses knew, as hard as it seemed, that this was truth from God. He said this to Aaron because these were his sons who did this and got this, not non-Aaronic people as in the case of Korah in Numbers 16. They were authorized priests, but they thought they knew better than God. They brought the wrong fire (verse 1).

Why did they do that? I don't know. I don't think it says. They apparently thought they had a way to do it, and they were going to do it that way.

What was the fire? Something possibly paralleling pagan practice? Possibly. The point isn't what it was. The point is what it wasn't. It wasn't what God had ordered.

Moses spoke to Aaron. Most of the time in such an embarrassing situation nobody says anything. How can you address an issue of someone's sons going so far off track?

Moses gets it back to God. What happened did not happen by chance. Nor was it a momentary conniption fit on God's part. God had told them this would happen. This was not, then, a 1984-style betrayal of a parent by a child in the grip of political correctness. This was absolute. Strange fire they offered in verse 1 and fire in verse 2 was what they got.

What Yahweh spoke... I looked this up in cross references and again in concordances, and I couldn't find a reference. It could be that this is something that Yahweh said in the past which is only now being quoted much like the quote of Jesus about giving in Acts 20. Even if this wasn't recorded earlier, it is still from the Lord as spoken to Moses personally or directly.

Man does not fall to judgment without adequate warning. Even people who don't have the scriptures have creation as Paul pointed out in Romans 1 and what C. S. Lewis called "The Tao" in his book, The Abolition Of Man. The moral fabric is there. Even people who reject it still talk about what is "right". They've redefined the category, but they regard it as a legitimate category.

God never calls us to account for what He has not delineated. He set a boundary in Eden. Then, people kept dying because of the sentence of death as we are told in Romans 5:12. In the law, God set an even greater boundary. That boundary is still in place as Paul tells us in Romans 7:7.

The law still defines sin. It is the judgment of the law that has been set aside, not the righteousness of the law. It was not removed because it was passé or found to be wrong. Colossians 2:14 sets out the truth on that.

The law traps us by its definitions. The trap is open and not covered over by brush keeping us from seeing what we will stumble into. Christ frees us by His blood. But the word of God is still true, even in our case.

By those who come near to me is a reference to a particular class, the priests. You get a driving license, and you can drive wherever you want as long as it is on the roads going the right way at the right speed. You cannot drive over the lawn, through the flower beds, right into the living room through the big plate glass window. The priests couldn't just approach god however they felt like it. They had to follow the rules.

The people, if we think in terms of where they physically went with regard to the tabernacle or the holy of holies, stayed far away from God. Earlier, they had operated under the prohibition against approaching Mt. Sinai.

God was in their midst, but not to become a thing or a "person" taken for granted.

Only certain people could come near. Not just everyone had a right to decide to come near.

The priests came near by bringing sacrifices and by the showbread (Leviticus 24:1-9). The High Priest came the nearest of all on the Day of Atonement. Even though he had the right to come near, he couldn't just come any time he pleased.

We are used to a society where those in power invent the rules for themselves as they go along. You saw this parodied quite clearly in the film "Bang The Drum Slowly" in which every town the ball team went to they would get into a game with locals which they called TEGWAR. That stands for The Exciting Game Without Any Rules. In other words, they always won, and those they played against always lost a lot of money. In real life I knew a person who, as an adult, bragged about the fact that when they played games with their brothers, they would always change the rules in the middle of the game so that they would win.

Nadab and Abihu thought that was them. Like mad scientists, they liked their fire and wanted to promote it. God, rather than being mean, merely called the rules on them.

Rules can be good. The fence and moat protect us from the lion at the zoo. The rules, when we keep on the right side of them, protect us from the wrath of God.

"I will be treated as holy," says Yahweh. We're talking about Yahweh here. He is holy, but we have seen that even though someone is president, he's still not treated as president, not just in recent days, but throughout the history of our country. In recent days of the 2019 entry a foreign ruler basically announced a death contract on the president of the United States. Even if that would be successful, it wouldn't be right.

In God's case, no one will be successful in treating God as anything but holy. The name of God alone should make this happen. If you only treat God as common or as a human construct, you will suffer for it.

They were afraid of profaning the name of God, yet I feel it would have been better to pronounce it and restrain yourself from sin rather than to not pronounce the name so as to avoid misusing it. You can not drive your car, and that will keep you from getting in an accident, but it won't get you or anyone else anywhere. They didn't really want to control their lips, so they took an easy way.

When we know Yahweh, we know how we must treat him. How can we treat God? Here are some potential ways (I do not vouch for any but the first, although I think men at various times have done all of these and more):

➢ As God, Lord, Yahweh, Creator.
➢ As a fixture in the universe, as if He were a distant star that had been charted, but which made no difference to our lives.
➢ As an equal.
➢ As a useless relic of the past.
➢ As a cultural figure of the imagination.

➢ As a mythic explanation for what cannot be explained.

➢ As man's invention.

The ways of mistreating God are multitudinous. There is only one right way to treat Him - with respect and obedience. That's the first way listed above. We treat God as holy by doing it His way. It's not that He is selfish, but that He knows the right way. In the adventure movies, it's always the fellow who won't follow the guide who disappears into the quicksand. Doing it His way is not testimony to His unreasonableness, but to His being what He says He is.

He is holy - separate, distinct, not like any other, pure, not for common use, permanent and not temporary. We treat God as holy when we don't think we know better.

No one knows better than God. No one can afford to leave God out of the calculations of his life.

We have something additional. Besides what they do, this truth is in place. God could not afford to let this strange fire pass, not because He was arrogated or prideful, but because it would not be good for us. If we trusted in our own means and ended up in hell that would be the greatest cruelty God could effect.

This is not only the priests. They got to come near to the extent of the Holy Place and, in the case of the high priest once a year, the Holy of Holies. Those who don't get past the gate with their offerings are responsible, too.

This was done before all people. The priests were not private individuals, but those whose acts affected and influenced and spoke for the entire people **and** for God. God will not allow Himself to be misrepresented by His priests, even today. The Christian is to act above board before the world. we're not to operate on the basis that because the world is evil we don't have to be straightforward with them. There is to be nothing out of us that makes God even appear as less than what He is.

God will be honored. He will be lifted up. This is not lip service, but following god. It's as many as are led by the Spirit of God who are in real relationship with God. (Romans 8:14)

Lifting up God is the only way to lift up ourselves. It is the only thing to do which is consistent with our nature as created beings. Evolution and Existentialism are wrong, but the worst of them is the effect they have on our acts rather than philosophies themselves. They encourage us to be our own gods, writing our own scriptures as we go (postmodernism), enacting our own laws, setting our own standards, finding our own way.

We cannot even keep the standards we set for ourselves without outside help. God calls us to honor Him because it enables us. Honor appears among the many ascriptions of God and Jesus in the book of Revelation five times. It is ascribed to both of them.

We are enabled to make moral choices because of God. Even if Dostoyevsky didn't say it, it's true: If there is no God, all things are possible, meaning all things that acts. Further, I would add, if all things are possible to the unaided will of man, then nothing is possible. Without form there is no existence. Even an amoeba has a "skin". Oh, I know there are disembodied spirits, but in the New Testament they always seem to want to find a body. That's a side note, though.

The point is that honoring God is not only appropriate to Him, but it's appropriate to us as well. It fits in with both our natures. Honor doesn't mean merely a salute in passing. If the soldier saluted the general and then refused to go into battle on orders, the salute would be mockery rather than meaningful. People think that because God is so big they can disappear in the crowd.

I know crowds. I've been in a lot of them over the years. Every time you went to Disneyland you were in a crowd. I was pressed severely in a political event where a candidate came and shook hands with everyone. I passed out tracts in a parade in San Francisco in the fall of 1969 which put, if I remember the figure right, about a million people on the streets. I was in the crowd that gridlocked part of Los Angeles county during walking in the protest against the release of the film, "The Last Temptation Of Christ". I was in a crowd of cars outside Angel Stadium in Anaheim, California, for over an hour waiting for all the Promise Keepers who wouldn't let anyone else get out of the parking lot ahead of them. In all these cases the crowds were so thick at times that it didn't seem like you were getting anywhere. It also seemed as though you shrunk in insignificance so that like "The Incredible Shrinking Man" of the film of the same name, no one knew you were there. You were an element of the crowd. What the mob did was apart from what you were, even though you were a part of them.

But... Think about this. All the crowds, and I still got separated out of them and back home, and so did everyone else. Our individual nature was preserved. I never disappeared in them. I never disappear before God. That should motivate and shape my actions.

The end result at this time was that Aaron kept silent like Job. He didn't question God. He didn't try to justify his boys. When God has spoken there is no room for debate, at least not on such things as this. Abraham "argued" with God over judgment, that is over a specific sentence. He never would have argued over definitions. He didn't say, "Commute their sentence," or re-define their sin so as to let them live. His understanding was that that was absolute.

So many want to argue with God over the absolutes. They want a recount. I saw a senate candidate call for and get a recount only to be disappointed. Rather than seeming like a power, he seemed like a baby. Man wants to be a power, though, so without leaving the church, or so he thinks, he changes thing around. We see that in the higher criticism of the past and the gender rhetoric of the present. They not only fall themselves when they do this, but they lead millions astray as well.

To be silent is not to be inactive. Aaron had already accepted the investiture described in Leviticus 8:10-13. He needed to learn the right way to carry out his mission.

There are times when we need to be silent before God. Even a fool can seem wise as Proverbs 17:28 points out by just shutting his mouth. A Danny Kaye character in the movie "On The Rivera" closed a business deal for billions of francs by just keeping his mouth shut.

When we are silent, God can speak and tell us what to do next. We can hear Him or we can just go ahead and do what we know to do already anyway.

When we quit questioning God we can act for God, not because we are know-nothings, but because we have accepted God's rule and authority and will.

God acts for the wholehearted and pure because that's how He is. How are we?

Look to God, not the crowd. The crowd noise in the background makes you know it is a live recording, but in the end, it's not the cough that makes the difference, but the playing of the musicians. Let God make the music.

God's direction.

Jacob didn't always do all right without direction. He bought the birthright when God had already foretold it to his mother. He cheated for the blessing, again when he didn't need to. He ran away for his life. He wasn't real marriage savvy in terms of the customs of his in-laws.

Here, he's starting to follow god instead of preceding Him. Spiritual etiquette means God goes through the door **first**. **Then**, we follow.

God spoke to Jacob. That's not the issue here, though. The question is, is God heard?

From verses 2 and 3 we know Jacob did hear.

God is going to get Jacob going. He says, "Arise." It's so easy to stay put, but it can be dangerous. I can remember a Mike Warnke album in which he talked about his time in Vietnam. He spoke of wanting to dally in a cool valley only to be told by wiser heads that it was exactly there that the enemy liked to pick people off. The pleasure of the location was a lure which became a trap. From the fact that he told the story we know he got up and got out of there.

The devil likes to see God's people go nowhere. God likes to see His people go **Higher**.

Jacob was at this time in or rather in front of Shechem. (Genesis 33:18) His boys got into big trouble with the locals because his girl wanted to be "sociable" where she shouldn't have been. Even Elly May Clampett wasn't so naïve that she was lured into the things Dinah (the daughter) was.

At this time there was no "outreach" being done by God's people. It was all they could do to be faithful to God themselves. Mostly, though, they had no good news to give out because none had been commissioned. They couldn't even say what we're doing and you'll get what we get. They were in a private program closed to outsiders at the time. The most important thing in such a setting is to attempt to stay close to God yourself. That's not our only item on the agenda, but it is still on our agenda as Christians. Put on your oxygen mask before assisting others.

Jacob needed to get to where God was at the time, and he was told where that was. Bethel means House of God. It wasn't an arbitrary pin stuck in the map, but the place where god had spoken to Jacob in the dream with the angels on the ladder. I was always fascinated by those angels going up and down when I heard this story as a kid. I'd seen escalators in the downtown department stores, but nothing like what

Jacob saw.

Sometimes people categorize such things as Jacob's dream under the heading: Religious Experiences. The experience is something you alone had, and it was not something that you could repeat at will. It was kind of like the old days when you didn't have a dvd to pop in, so if you were going to see something you had to depend on the station broadcasting and your finding out about it and being at home at the time as well.

God is not calling us to a spectacular gala extravaganza which will be a high experience which will be over the next day. He is calling us to live with Him. (Well, I guess that is a spectacular gala extravaganza.)

To go to the house of God and live there is to be where you can keep an eye on God and see what he's up to and get in on it. I'm not saying we should all move into the church building, but that we should live in the presence of God to such an extent that only what God thought mattered to us. So many people "go to church", but they live their lives elsewhere.

With the Holy Spirit in us we are to live our lives in the House of God because we are the House or Temple of God.

Jacob is not just to settle down, but to be in relationship to God. That's what building an altar is all about. It's to get in on the sacrifices which maintain relationship with God. We don't have an account spelling out what those were at this time like we do 500 plus years later during the time of Moses, but Jacob knew, even if we don't.

Just because we don't know everything that Jacob did exactly doesn't mean we cannot apply this to ourselves. We, too, are to be involved in sacrifices which maintain relationship with God. The New Testament speaks of these in I Peter 2:5 and Hebrews 13:15-16. We don't just build an altar. We are the altar, especially in the sacrifices mentioned in Hebrews. We don't save ourselves, but we offer the sacrifices of praise and peace.

The altar is **to** God. It's not merely a beautiful artifact. It is functional.

There was no doubt about who this God was. He was the one who had appeared to Jacob before. Many years ago I prepared and preached a message called "GYOG". It's not a word, but it was an acronym for "Get Your Own God". That's what Jacob needed to do. Most of the time in his life he referred to God as the God of his father. At the end, though, he called God his own God. We all need to make that shift, especially if we have grown up in the church. When you appear before the throne no one's faith matters before God but your own. Your father's God will not save you unless He is your god. Everyone has to have his own ticket for his own seat. You can't sit on anyone's lap.

God didn't have to be discovered or invented. He revealed Himself. He didn't stand in the shadows. He wasn't like a monster in a movie shown only partially in the dark and in a flash of movement so you don't really get a good look at it because if you saw him clearly he wouldn't be all the frightening or even silly. In this case, God shows Himself in full light and lets us have a good look. In Jesus He showed us Himself so we can know the real full person.

Jacob knew who this was. God is not an unknown god, but a Known God. He did something with Jacob once he got there in verses 6-12. God made promises to Jacob and changed his name and gave him a mission and a possession.

Going to God's house is not a side show. It's the center ring, and everything else stops when God acts.

Genesis 48:15-16
19 January 2019

We need to be blessers. This will change us as much as the blessed ones.

When we speak of a blessing, we are neither talking about an unsupported wish or magic. Some blessings in scripture were prophetic, but you don't have to be a prophet to utter a blessing. The blessing is the loosing of God on the person in the direction set forth in the blessing.

Verse 15

Jacob blessed Joseph. That's what it say, although he blesses Joseph by blessing his sons, much as Noah cursed Ham by cursing His son, Canaan.

We are tied into the entire family line. No man is an island. John Donne had it right.

Joseph had been the favored son, but it was Judah who got the line of the Messiah due to wrongdoing of the three ahead of him. Still, just because we don't do one blessing doesn't mean we don't do one at all.

The blessing begins with the source. It is described in three ways – two here and one in the next verse.

1.   The God before whom my Fathers Abraham and Isaac walked.

We don't ever need a new God. Nothing happens to the old one. He's never worn out or outmoded or superseded. God, by definition, is eternal. Eternal, by definition, is always, never ending.

Jacob knew both his fathers and their God. Both Abraham and Isaac were alive in Jacob's early days, although there's no record of any interaction with Abraham. The generations seem to be compartmentalized. Still, he had plenty of time to see how these men related to God. There was no doubt that Yahweh was their God. They didn't hide it.

God is the one before whom you should walk. Adam lost out when he didn't walk with God. God didn't tell him he couldn't walk before Him. That's what he thought himself. I wonder what might have been different if, instead of hiding and blameshifting, he'd come out and confessed at the very beginning? There would still have been consequences, but they might have been different.

These men their own wrong doing, but they were always open before God. The fathers walked before God. They were capable of being before Him. So, this says as much of them as it does of God. You can only walk before God when you're walking God's way.

108

It's the Lord, not the people who is the root of the blessing. God is the root of every blessing. We can walk before God. we do this, not only in going to church, but every day. There's never a time when we're not walking before God.

2.　　　　The God who has been my shepherd all my life to this day.

God is not localized. He is neither a God of the hills nor a God of the plains, but simply God everywhere.

God is now Jacob's God. The Lord is my shepherd. Jacob said this almost 1000 years before David did.

God has been my shepherd. He has a record in my life. There's no wondering about it.

The shepherd leads, provides, protects, but he doesn't move the sheep around like pieces on a chessboard. The Greek god Zeus is depicted as doing that in the film, "Clash Of The Titans." Actually, I think there are times when we wish we could do that or else when we wish that God would pick us up and put us down in the place of our choosing, but He doesn't do things that way.

God is wiling to take care of us, but are we following Him, going in and out, eating in His pasture or are we going astray each his own way?

Jacob had covered a lot of ground in his life. He had cheated and deceived, but God met him and took him on.

However, God didn't make everything happen that happened in this story. God didn't cheat Jacob like Laban did. he didn't throw women at him. Jacob and others did that on their own at times. It was the overall arching picture that God painted. He provided and made a nation out of Jacob. Somehow, we don't know all the details, God was behind the spotted/striped sheep and goats in Genesis 31:9-13.

God can only be my shepherd when I let Him.

Jacob acknowledges that God was always there. This was true all his life. God never left Jacob even when Jacob did wrong things. That doesn't endorse the wrong. it shows the faithfulness of God. If we are faithless, He remains faithful as Paul says of Jesus in II Timothy 2:13.

Verse 16

3.　　　　The angel who has redeemed me from all evil.

I don't think he's calling God an angel. He's recognizing that God's angel acted for God. That's a bold statement to make in a world where everything has to have a natural cause. It is insightful. It is perceptive. It sees beyond this life.

This shows a legitimate relationship. Angels don't do things on their own apart from the direction of God. They are ministers to us (Hebrews 1:14). It's not, though, that he's asking the angel to do anything, but that he knows that the angel did this on his behalf.

He redeemed **me** from all evil. I got in evil, but I was bought out. no evil shall rule over God's people. They may be in it for a time, but God redeems His own. He always pays off our pawn ticket.

All evil is every thing evil that happened to him, not just a few things. We can't think up anything that God can't get us out of.

The Blessing Part

Bless the lads – Ephraim and Manasseh. They're specifically blessed by Jacob in verse 20. Here it's God who is requested to do this.

Bless my children. Extend yourself in them, Elohim.

Bless their children. This would be my name living on through them. It's not that our name is the big thing, but that what God has done with us should continue on. We only have a right to expect something of ourselves to live on in our descendents if that something is something of God.

It's not only Jacob, but Abraham and Isaac who he wants to have live on. This means that the life of God is living in them.

The and gives us the mission. He is to grow to a multitude in the midst of the earth. This is not Jacob's agenda, but his acknowledgment of God's earlier promise to Abraham. He does not forget what God said to his grandfather. We always need to remember what God has said to those have gone on before us because it applies to us as well. Jacob is not going to break the chain. This is something he has a right to put into others.

We want what comes after us to grow into something greater. We want God to be the measure of its possibility, not ourselves.

This is a place not to be content. We are not to be like King Louis XV of France who said, "Apres moi, le deluge" which is translated as "After me, the flood." The idea was that he knew the revolution was coming, but it wouldn't come until after he was off the scene. He didn't do anything to try to stem it or change the government or have his descendents bow out so they wouldn't be beheaded. He just let it come. We are not to let the flood come if we can open up the blessing on God to stop it.

I want God in our family to be greater. I want God in our church to be greater. I want God in our journaling group to be greater. None of these are because they are what I want, but because it's what God wants.

We ought to be open to pasing blessings on rather than hoarding them up. They're meant to be bequeathed to those coming along after us.

What I want to bequeath is what has already been given to me:

110

- ❖ Salvation
- ❖ The indwelling Holy Spirit
- ❖ Eternal Life
- ❖ The way
- ❖ The word
- ❖ Love

God is going to do something beyond us and beyond our time.

Leviticus 17:11
11 February 2013

This is the only legitimate use for blood, besides in our body.

The only true theology is blood theology. That's because blood is the only thing so absolutely connected with life. According to the Bell Telephone special of the 1950s called "Hemo The Magnificent", inside our body the blood stream has access to every cell. That makes it both necessary and significant.

This verse is sandwiched between two verses dealing with God's judgment on human consumption of blood. This is later reversed, not in the literal sense, but in the spiritual sense of our participation in the blood of Jesus through the Lord's supper.

The life of the flesh is worked through the blood to such an extent that it is called the life of the flesh. The body has no life in itself. Bare meat is unendowed. Blood only works in the flesh because it circulates, but the life principle is there.

Life. We're getting real basic here. This is animal life, but also innocent life. In sacrifice only innocent blood can provide forgiveness. Animals are innocent. They cannot sin. When it comes to men, only Jesus has ever been sinless. He did not sin.

The life is what has been given. God didn't hold His life to Himself, but shared it. He says He has given it, past tense.

It depends on where the blood is what it does for you. If you eat it, you're cursed. If it gets on you, you're guilty as we see in verses 15-16. If it's on the altar, it cleanses.

God gives outright to you personally on the altar. This is the greatness of God. He didn't just make us, but He made provision for us, even when we did what was wrong.

Christmas gifts would still be gifts, even if they weren't under the tree or were given at other times, but this is only a gift on the altar. It can't be such anywhere else. It is only good in a sacrificial context. It has to be offered to God to do you any good.

How strange, though. That would be like Gorge eating a chocolate bar and I get the taste and gain the weight, but that is how it works.

God is very particular. It's life He's giving. You don't fool around with that. It's like a transfusion bag given to someone in the hospital. There are two people in the room when it is put into the patient. They mark it off that it's what the doctor ordered and the right blood for the recipient. The blood of Jesus is the only right blood for us now, but then the blood of the animal worked within the confines of the sacrificial system.

The life that is in the blood is innocence. This comes to us on the cross, the altar of which the others have no right. (Hebrews 13:10)

It makes atonement. There was a Mexican restaurant near where I grew up that featured tacos. They sign outside said, "See 'Em Made". This was in the days when tacos were not the staple they are now. There also used to be establishments that advertised that they could service whatever was needed "While You Wait". There is no doubt of this for it is made while we are there, not in the Holy of Holies, but while we are in attendance. We couldn't be at the cross, but in our baptism this happens.

God cannot overlook sin. He has to cover it. this covers our sols so that He does not see the sin. Our souls are covered so that we can approach God.

Atonement is not a light thing, but an event of full effect. It's a happening which makes things happen.

God is interested in us as persons, that is as souls, not merely as statistics. He doesn't count us, but we count with Him. He does this for us, not because our sin made Him look bad for making a creature that sinned, but so that we could have the blessing of being cleansed.

Almost more is said about the Day of Atonement than any other sacrificial day except probably the Passover. The Passover had to come first. God had to get the people out of bondage before He could cover their sin. Pharaoh thought it a mere whim or a scheme, but here we see that they **needed** to get away. We have to get out of sin to be saved. We won't be saved in our sin.

God releases us, not to sin again, but to be free of sin. He doesn't just put His brand on us, and then let us loose, but He enters us as Christians. This has a physical base – blood.

There was a company in the Northwest when I was growing up that plastered their motto all over billboards over town. They said of their beer, "It's the water." Now, I've never tasted their beer or any other, but I rather like God saying, "It's the blood." I like that much better.

Blood is employed by reason of the life. Even the blood alone is not the point. it is the life which the blood contains which is the point. This life is what makes atonement.

Something which is dead cannot do anything for you. That which is alive can.

God gives life. He tries to keep us from losing life. He points out both the cliff and the path. People we know tell us all the obstacles. God tells us the way and the end arrived at.

Life.

Leviticus 11:45
9 February 2015

Why they are not to be unclean and to consecrate themselves. That's what we are told. There is always a balance between what to be and what not to be. The fulcrum is the Lord.

For gives us the reason. I am the Lord. I, and no one else, am the Lord. God is not afraid to say, "I." I don't remember such pronouncements in what I read of the ancient pagan myths. There the "gods" did what they wanted, but didn't address man. Our God speaks to us.

All this is about His existence. I Am Yahweh. God doesn't have to do anything to be. He doesn't have to become to be. He did because He was. The past tense is from our point of view only, not His.

He is the Yahweh, the specific being, the one, the only Lord. he is always ahead of us. He is preceding in every particular of creation.

God asks us to act because of who He is. There is no other basis for morality. Social relations have no base for right and wrong. If it's all about society ruling, I give you the Nazis and the Bolsheviks as poster children for that route. Morality is not created by majority or plurality or power. God is the standard. The God standard works where the gold standard is not capable of working.

How did they know He was the Lord? by what He did for them. God brought them up. They could not have walked out if God had not sent the plagues.

God did not intend that they come out, but that they should come up. Up to Sinai.

People only knew the standards of God in a vague way until Sinai. I know Gospel is better than Law, but Law was better than no law and still being punished for doing wrong as we see in Romans 5:13-14. it's better to know.

God brought them up. He raised them up. They came up from:

❖ Slavery
❖ Ignorance
❖ Sin
❖ Lack of identity
❖ Being a part of Egypt
❖ The wiles of Pharaoh (midwives, no straw, denying his word, etc.)

God doesn't take anyone anywhere but up.

The land of Egypt had once been their provision when they had first gone to Goshen. The provision of the past is not intended to be the God of the present. That's the problem they created later in worshipping the bronze serpent. Past provision needs to be moved on from. It can prove a present trap.

God had given them a land – Canaan. The earlier Pharaoh had given them Goshen, but that wasn't the land God wanted them to have. I've always wondered why they didn't go back, either after the famine crisis had passed or after Joseph had died, but they didn't.

God can take us out of wherever we are or wherever we have been put. God took them out of Egypt. Egypt would have been a bad influence. It was a land of idolatry, a land of a Big Slave Buffet (featuring cucumbers, leeks, onions and garlic), a place to forget about God.

God wanted them to come out and sacrifice to remember Him. That was the initial request. I don't think God would have left them there forever, but if Pharaoh had cooperated, he would have saved himself and his family and his nation a lot of grief. Pharaoh had his own terms for their exiting the country, and they couldn't do it on his terms.

God brought them out so He could be their God, not Horus or Baste or any of the others. People knew the names of those "gods," but I never read that anyone claimed to know any of them.

God wanted to be the God of Israel and to be known by Israel. That would be like some celebrity wanting to be our celebrity to be known by our name. Can you imagine John Wayne being known as the movie star of Kevin Levellie. Where's the box office draw in such a designation? That sort of thing is unthinkable. They want us to be their fans, but not for them to be ours. They don't want to belong to us.

God wants to belong to us. It's not that we control Him or call the shots, but that we have an exclusive relationship to Him.

Because of this God had a Holy Equation:

You holy – I Holy

V

Because

of

the

Balancing

Word

They were to be set apart from Egypt and all the other nations. Constantly through Moses and Joshua they were told not to be a part of those nations, not to marry into them, not to be connected to them.

We can only be holy because Yahweh is holy. That is not a wish or a "Manifest Destiny". It is the purpose for deliverance. It is the same in the new covenant.

If you are not delivered, you don't have a purpose. Sin has no purpose. God has one. It's for you. You are to be like Him.

No one ever aspired to be like the Egyptian "god" Ra that I ever heard of. It was the same with Canaanite, Greek, Roman, Indian, Chinese and Norse "gods". This is a unique feature of God's people. The other "gods" probably wouldn't have wanted people to be like them. In Ray Harryhausen's film, "Jason And The Argonauts", Jason is told that the gods like those best who help themselves, in other words, they like those who don't call on them.

That is not our God. he wants to be called on. He wants to be in conference with us.

God delivers so we may be something. How many people, ever, want you to be something or have told you that? Sometimes, they say, "Make something of yourself," but, "Be Something"? Only our God says that. Jesus says the same.

The Being God want being fellowship with being people. believing is the way to get to be being.

Deuteronomy 13:4
10 March 2018

Who is speaking here? Go back to 5;1. they have quotes as if Moses said all this except for the "Thus saith the Lord" parts. Moses says this directly to the people. He's not prophesying, but exhorting.

You is who here. No one else will do. He is giving the positive follow up to the negative about what they were to do regarding a false prophet. It's still good for us. If we do this, no amount of false prophets will derail us.

You shall follow. It's up to you, but you should do this.

We can think of following the leader as in the children's game. It could be imitating someone when they say "Walk this way," as William Powell did in "Another Thin Man" where he copied the walking style of the butler. It had better be, "Follow me as I follow Christ" as Paul put it in I Corinthians 11:1.

To follow is to come after. A follower doesn't blaze a trail. He takes the trail shown to him. In our case, this is not merely the road less traveled but, as Jesus put it, the narrow way.

When we follow Jesus, we don't have time to think about where we **didn't** go. When we follow Jesus, we get to where Jesus is. Here it is the Lord your God or Yahweh your Elohim.

They had followed the pillar in the wilderness, but they were not going to have that. they would nee to follow the world of the God rather than the manifestation of God. we're walking in the same shoes.

He sets the pace and sets the place. God doesn't go everywhere. There is a moral way and a host of immoral ways. Jesus went to all sorts of places, but He never went their way. It was always His way, but He invited the others to follow that way.

God is not static in heaven. He is moving. God doesn't just walk the dark hills; He walks in this world. He walks to our church. He walks to our world. He walks to our market. He walks to our living room.

We are to fear as well as follow. That is, we are to focus on who we are following.

I can play the piano without looking at the keys. Ray Charles and George Shearing could do that, too, even though they were blind. But, no one can follow God without looking. We have to see Him and nothing but Him.

Fear is like blinders that shut out every other sight which might try to pull us or guide us. Fear means that we are only impressed by God and His wisdom. We don't have time for anyone else. Confucius may say, but God guides, and I follow and fear. Fear means I pay

117

attention to Him.

Now we look at four things to do because we are following and fearing.

1.   Keep His commandments

It's not just the ten. Sometimes people refer to them as though they were the totality of what anyone needed to do. Jesus spoke of teaching those who were made disciples to keep the commandments. He reduced them at one point to two, but in those two lie everything that is to be done.

To keep the commandments is to keep them all – James 2:10. you can't do a majority of them or 50% + 1. You keep them by doing them, not by thinking them or posting them on a well.

Even if they take down the ten commandments from every public place in the world, that will not affect us. It may affect the world by giving some people the idea that there are no rules. They will have a rude awakening to the true reality on the day of judgment, but it won't hurt the Christian, only the one who has not come to Jesus. The lack of these in the public arena will take away the testimony of God and hurt people who are deceived into thinking there is no moral base, but we sill still be keeping the commandments.

2.   Listen to His voice

You'd think this would be first. We learn on the job.

We listen when we are orientated to listen. We are orientated by our action.

Listen means to take in. It is more than hearing. We can hear without listening. "What was that?" We heard, but we didn't listen or else we wouldn't have to ask the question.

Fear is focusing ourselves on one place only. Listening is the same. It is like a radio tuned into a very particular frequency. It doesn't gawk around at everything. It listens to the one station. It doesn't try to listen to all the stations at once. I don't know that there is a radio which could do that, but even if there was, it wouldn't do anyone any good because they couldn't take in thousands or of songs and speeches and announcements all at once. There is no bleed over from any other station as sometimes happens with a radio. The signal of God is so strong that no other signal will share the frequency with it, and we are not to attune ourselves to others while we hear it.

3.   Serve Him

People want to have or know God, but doing something for Him? That's a horse of a different color.

We serve God, not by what we do to Him, but by what we do for Him. To serve God is to magnify ourselves rather than to diminish ourselves. It makes us more than what we would be otherwise.

Think of the people of faith we admire. Think if they had no faith and had just done what they did alone.

Serving God shows that you fear God and follow Him and listen to Him. this shows that you pass the test.

4.   Cling to Him

Perseverance. This is not something God does, but something **we** do.

Don't let go. Hold on. We hold on by doing all the things ahead of this.

When we cling we become that which cannot be removed. When we hold on, God will hold us. Even if we are killed as martyrs, we will not lose our grip. It will be strengthened.

Moses is calling the people to be more than a political movement or unity. He is calling them to be God's people. This is the same for us.

We need to:
❖ Follow
❖ Fear
❖ Keep
❖ Listen
❖ Serve
❖ Cling

We start by following. Then, when times get hard we just hold on. We cling. No matter what prophet or preacher comes along, cling.

These are what we are to do.

Numbers 23:19
27 February 2016

Before getting into this passage, I want to do a little thinking out loud on paper about some things. God didn't actually literally repent in Genesis 6:6 even though the American Standard Version says that it repented Him that He made man. He changed His mind about man and what he was going to do with him. We discussed some of this in the entry on Genesis 6:6 and will do more in this one, but we need to get this straight. God did not wipe all men out like man would have done if he had been in charge of the program. He merely started with a new group made out of the best of the old group, but he did not turn from man. He just redid the relationship. The institution of man went on. So much for man, but what about God?

God is not a man. Whatever we say about the character and nature of man cannot be said about God. Man is made in God's image, but God is the reference point, not man. We would never say that God is a reflection of the image He made in man. God is the reflection of no one. He is light, not a mirror. We begin here with the absolute otherness of God.

The next part of this is not so much a definition of man as it an observation of the observed practices of man. Man lies. God does not lie. There's no occasion in which God would ever lie. I know about the story of the lying spirit, but that was God using a spirit such as Ahab himself would have employed to speak to Ahab. Micaiah, the true prophet of the true God, told Ahab that what was being told him had its source in a lying spirit. He exposed the lie and told the truth. That should have stopped Ahab from going to battle, but he went and lost his life. God did not lie there or anywhere else.

This doesn't mean that man by nature is a liar, but that He is, by virtue of free will, capable of lying. God is not. See Hebrews 6:18.

God and man are not in the same category. There is a God, and I am not Him. I originally heard that in a camp sermon, but a few years later it was quoted in a movie. I don't know the original source. I looked on the internet. I found people cited who used to say this, but so far no author, so I'd say it's in the public domain. It's not scripture, but it's a good summary.

We are not to reduce God to our level. That's what J. B. Phillips was saying in his book <u>Your God Is Too Small</u>.

Balak here thought that God could be controlled. He had to be disabused of that idea.

To not lie means that He tells only the truth. God is not

deceptive. The nature of God precludes deception. God can only tell the truth. The Ahab story cited earlier illustrates that. God used the lying spirit there as He used the Chaldeeans in Habakkuk. That didn't justify lying or killing. It was only a judgment mechanism. God used the very things men admired – deception and power – to destroy them.

The son of man here is not a reference to Jesus, but simply to one whose nature is human. Man can repent because of free will. he has to repent because he has sinned. God has free will, but no sin. Jesus showed that it is possible to have free will without sin.

Balak needed to know that God was not going to go back on His people. That's where we started in this entry.

Once God has made a pronouncement, He holds to it more surely that the Medes and the Persians did to their un-set-asideable law.

God knows all things. Knowing them, He has no cause to repent. The regret of Genesis 6 was an anguish of heart, not a change of plan. Genesis 6 shows that God will not save man in his sin. He made man, but He does not love him so much that He ever says, "My creation, right or wrong." His holiness is balance to His love and both are balanced by grace and mercy or we might say by motivation and realization.

God is not going to damn Israel, taking Israel in the full definition of the term which it is given in Romans and Galatians. He is not going to damn those who are in Christ no matter what the world does or thinks about them.

Has He said... Those are almost the same words the serpent used. In that case they were words of doubt. Here they are words of affirmation.

God declared Himself to Abraham, Isaac, Jacob and then to Moses and to the whole people at Sinai. God will never say, "I didn't mean it" or "I was just joking."

Will He not do it? NO! He will do it.

The pronouncements of God will be. That's why we can hope in the unseen. We believe the one who said these things.

The world thinks they have supplied us with reasons for not believing. True, they provide no reasons for believing **them**, but God supplies reason for believing in Him.

Whatever God said He will do. It's not that it will be done, which would be passive, but that He will do it, which is active.

The word, "or" gives us a parallelism. The question is asked in alternate terms, but it's the same question getting the same answer. It just reinforces the answer given.

Has He spoken and will He not make it good? Whatever God says, he will do.

Turning the first part of this from a question into a statement we have: He is not silent. God has expressed Himself. He's not left us hanging or wondering.

How can we even question whether God will make it good or not? People can and do say anything. That doesn't mean you'll get it from them. That's not how it is with God.

Whatever the world makes of it, God will make it good. Whatever we make of it, God will make it good. Whatever God said, He will make it good.

God fulfills. He never makes evil. He never gives evil gifts. Jesus made that clear in Luke 11:13.

The world was made by God and pronounced good by God. God knows good when He sees it. He doesn't know evil on any experiential level. He doesn't know how to make evil.

God judges all by good, not by good and evil. Evil is not a category in God' thinking, strictly speaking. Oh, He knows about it, but He didn't create it as a cataloger. Before the serpent it was not in the world, as far as I can tell from scripture.

We know nothing of the origin of Satan from scripture. He was called a liar from the beginning and a murderer from the beginning, but we know nothing else about him before he came into human experience. Nothing Satan does, however, can be ascribed, even remotely to God.

This is not dualism. As God is ant a man, neither is He a devil, not even a very clever one. Good is not a mild wimpy term taken as the negation of evil, but an absolute. A thing is good or it is not. If it is not, it does not matter what shade of ungood it is. it is not good.

We are to be concerned only with good. we learn the true bill, not the counterfeits. There is only one true bill. It is the counterfeits which are many.

Leviticus 22:32
13 February 2016

This comes at the end of a whole lot of distinctions between holy and unholy, clean and unclean.

This is not compartmentalized. It involves every part of life. Having said that, though, we are not to be "Holiness People" or "Love People" as though either one of those were the only character of God. We are to be God people, specifically Jesus people.

1.   You shall not profane my holy name.

The book of Leviticus is a handbook of sacerdotal services and regulations for the Levites, but it's also for the common people. Such things as this are still for us because they deal with general principles about God which will never be outdated. This never fails or fades.

We are responsible for what we do with God. we are not off the hook because of God's nature. He cannot be affected or infected by us. If He could be, then Jesus never could have come in the flesh.

We lose out when we live as if God were less than what He is.

There are chains of stores featuring the word "Less" in their names: Payless Shoes, Food 4 Less, etc. There is no God 4 Less. You can get Him for less and you'll get nothing less from Him than everything He has to give you. If you still want God 4 Less, though, you'll end up simply Godless in both your relationship to God and in your personal character.

To profane the name is to bring it down to a common level. It is to dirty it.

People are concerned with their "good name". In many cases, the goodness of the name is currency for success and profit.

Take two names – Rolls Royce and Edsel. The one is respected, the other not, although the Edsel wasn't a bad car. People and technicians just weren't ready for it. Their unreadiness is what gave it a bad name, which just goes to show that you can get a bad name from anywhere.

Let's never give God a bad name by our unreadiness to follow Him or obey Him.

Sadly, the world is more convinced by the fictional Elmer Gantry than they are by me. Elmer's unrighteousness makes them comfortable. They don't have to obey God if organized religion is just a sham for show, anyway. Our lives should never give people the idea that they don't have to obey God.

The name is all God is. we are never to even imply that He is less than He is. We are not to do this. We can praise or vilify human leaders without loss or gain to ourselves, but here there is a real loss if we do it.

Why are we not to profane the name? The but to come explains it.

2.   But I, God, will be sanctified among the sons of Israel.

Even in the Old Testament God was not content just to be in the temple. He was to be sanctified, i.e. set apart among the covenant people.

Christians are to live different lives than the world. we are to keep God sanctified in ourselves. He is set apart, holy, different.

Sanctified is a definite act. It's not a "state of mind". It's not a point of view or outlook or frame of reference. They sanctified God by refraining from sin and by sacrificing. They sanctified God by fulfilling the law.

What Jesus said about the sheep in Matthew 25 was really what they were supposed to be doing already. If you look at the law you see there the same commands to love your neighbor, provide for him, etc. You're even supposed to look out for his stray livestock. The social ethic is the same. It's only strengthened because we can now do it by the power of the indwelling Holy Spirit. But, we still have to be the ones doing it.

We sanctify now by our organic functioning in the church. When we do the gifts we show that we are sanctified. Sanctification is always for something. it is for something other than us.

Our lives are for God. God is for the Saints and the world. That pretty much covers it.

God is going to be sanctified among His people. The sons of Israel is a complete designation. All Israel will be saved. (Romans 11:26) No one who is in Israel can exempt himself from this. Here it is not we who sanctify, but God is sanctified in us. We've got to sweep the house out and have God fill it.

God will share space with no one. He is not an "ecumenical" God with Allah and Shiva and all the rest. He is the only God. He is one.

If God is one of many or first among equals, we have made Him nothing for we have denied every one of His claims. God only does us good if He is sanctified in us.

3.   How can this be? God is the one who does it.

He is the Yahweh who sanctifies you. Our will lets God do this, but He is the one who does it. as great as "good men" are, but are no good if God is not sanctified in them.

God identifies Himself by this function. We are often known by our function – husband, father, preacher, tax-payer, driver, etc. Those are some of my functions.

God is also known by what He does. This is not the ground of His being. This is His I Am-ness. This is our interface.

We can recognize a person from a distance by their walk, for example. We can't always break it down or even do it ourselves, but we know it's them when we see that walk. No one else walks like God does.

God is the one who does this. After the sacrifices they were cleansed. After the ashes of the red heifer they were cleansed. After the cross and our obedience (faith, repentance, confession, baptism) we are cleansed. We put ourselves in the way of God, and we'll be cleansed. Step out in front of a train, and you'll be killed. You can't help it. Step in the way of God, and you'll be cleansed. It happens.

God sanctifies us by removing all blame and guilt. He makes us ready for heaven. He makes it so that we can breathe there. We can stand face to Face. That's the power of sanctification.

I don't trust many "remedies" of man. I was helped over bronchitis by and antibiotic, but I've known people who weren't, and I've seen people with boxes full of pills who were worse than they would have been without them.

We are better than we could be with God.

We're not bad by nature, but limited. God makes us limitless. The action of God is on us and for us and about us. It's only "fair that we're about Him.

Deuteronomy 4:39
6 March 2016

We don't know the book of Deuteronomy like we should. It has a frame of reference and perspective beyond the first four books. It leads us directly to the New Testament, especially with it's declaration of 6:4 and the passage in chapter 30 quoted by Paul at length in Romans 10.

Know therefore today. This is something we are to do. It's not just something which comes to us out of the night or shows up in the afternoon mail. We are to know it.

The "therefore" is the funnel of all that has gone ahead. To know is an imperative. Knowledge doesn't "come" to a person or mushroom from an invisible spore in the brain. Even when we figure something out, it's because all the data from outside has come to us and we have in place a standard of evaluation by which we can order our thoughts. We have to be taught that. Romulus and Remus, Mowgli and Tarzan are pleasant fictions, but I don't think anyone could do what they did in the stories. They have found actual people in similar circumstances who have grown up only in a state of nature apart from human influence who have been totally ignorant. That's because wolves and apes don't teach people anything, and people don't learn without help.

I can't speak for Adam. Maybe God imprinted things on him. he seems to have come into existence knowing how to speak. Did Adam teach Eve or did she know? Theirs would be the only cases I can think of where people started their existence with at least some imprint of knowledge. They had to know those things because there was no other human being to feed them and take care of them.

We know, not just because we have been programmed a la Brave New World, but because we grasp what is given to us. We are to know it today, not mañana.

I have had to learn the difference between procrastination and pacing yourself. In college I wrote a paper attacking procrastination. It caused a stir among my procrastinating dorm neighbors who were in the same class. Now, I often do what I would have formerly called procrastination, but which is really a matter of timing and pacing.

Knowledge of this sort cannot be left until later because later may be too late. Jesus could come back or you could die. That's all it takes to remove you from the field of action. I don't know for sure, but a stroke might not keep you from willing to know something if it came within your reach, but there are conditions such as Alzheimer's which would also seem to preclude the ability to know even though a person was alive.

You have to know God today. You can't put off knowing Jesus. As Jesus challenged those He met along the way and as the apostles preached later in acts, there was never the idea that you could go home and think it over or sleep on it.

Today is always the only day we have.

Next, take it to heart.

Knowledge can never be surface only. It has to be internalized, and interned. We can't let it escape us.

A clever sign I once read said something along the lines of, "I already know everything. I just don't knew where I put it." That's why the old Sunday School teachers said that memorizing the reference was as important as memorizing the verse. You not only had to know what it said, but you needed to be able to tell people where it is so they can find it for themselves. In the sense of information alone it isn't, but in the sense of documentation it is. Nothing can be established without its credentials. The reference is the credential of the verse. God is the credential of the reference.

Take it to your heart – not your head, but your heart. In your heart you know he's right. Not enough voters took that slogan to heart and Barry Goldwater lost the race, but here it's not God who will lose, but you if you don't know it in your heart.

We take what we know where it should be.

The heart is the innermost part of us. I did a 16 week almost exhaustive sermon series on the heart. That is the most important place, yet we live on the surface and ignore the heart. We concentrate too much on acts alone. We concentrate on getting through and getting by.

Knowledge should be inside us. not pride or self or sin, but knowledge of God.

There will be a test, so it's good to know what knowledge it is we are to have.

We are to know that the Lord He is God.

Put in another way, this is to know that Yahweh (the personal name of God) is God (the designation of the being He is). You can't substitute on either side of the "is" equation. Nothing else is Elohim, and Yahweh is nothing other than God. That is not an empty tautology, but a Person and a Class. It is a class or category of only one, but it is still a legitimate class.

We need to live life with Yahweh as the point of reference. We need to know that we know Yahweh through Jesus. that is the only way. It's another way of saying that we know God through Himself.

We do not know God by other people's expressed knowledge of Him or by anyone's speculation of Him. True, even in scripture, we only see the tip top of the tip of the iceberg in this lifetime as far as coming to know everything there is to know about God is concerned, but we know that the rest of the iceberg is more of the same in relation to the top. In heaven and on earth covers it all.

C. S. Lewis was right. I don't know what work he said it in, but he basically claimed that there is no neutral ground in the universe. The devil lays claim to some (maybe even all) of it now, but his claim will be thrown out since everything is and always has been always God's.

This is my Father's world. It doesn't belong to the state of Illinois or the USA or any individual. No matter whose names are on the deeds in the recorders' offices, it all belongs to God.

Heaven – we have no problem with God's authority and ownership there. Only a fool would claim the supremacy in God's place. The atheists who don't believe in God and attempt to disprove what they "know" isn't there are only trying to raise themselves to godhood.

We can let no one take the place of heaven, and we can let no establish their claim to the earth. The earth doesn't even belong to itself or any of its creatures. Thus, the claim of the spotted owl, for example is OUT OF COURT. (I'm not advocating irresponsibility, but merely demonstrating that no one but God is in charge of creation.

There is no other. I've already said this, but I'll say it again. There is no other Elohim. The claims of others are put forth by their worshippers, but the "gods" make no claims for themselves. Our God does.

His name declares I Am, and every quality after that is declared by Him.

God is light.

God is love.

God is holy.

God is a jealous God. He has a right to be while we have no right to such jealousy other than perhaps in marriage against outsiders who would force their way in.

Everything else has a synonym or double. I've had people tell me I look just like "So and So", and at times they have even appealed to others to back up their opinion in the matter. I may look like thousands of people, but I am not any of those people. I am only myself.

Anyone who says that such and such a being or designation "looks like" God has not looked at God. There is no one. Not just no one like Him, not just no resemblance, but no one.

The singularity of God is the beginning of all doctrine. We have it in both testaments in Genesis 1:1 and John 1:1, e.g.

He will not share His glory with another. The claims of others are just claims. The claims of God are truth. They are the only reality.

There is no "alternate universe" to the universe of our God.

Leviticus 16:30
11 February 2019

The sacrifices of the pagans were to appease their "gods". It only did something for the people indirectly by not having the "gods" mad at them. It just removed an irritant, but didn't provide a positive benefit. This sacrifice does something for the people. That is a totally different concept, possibly even for the other sacrifices God's people had done before the law codified sacrifices.

Here's where man went from doing the best he could do to knowing what to do and what he would get for it.

Covering – cleansing – clean. That's the progression. We go from what happens to the sin to what happens to us to the state we get to be in.

This was the best, the most that could have been offered for people at the time, but without it everyone then living would have been stuck in Genesis 3.

There had been sacrifices from Adam to Moses, yet none appeared to be systematized as they were in the book of Leviticus. That was something new, even though to us it seems something incredibly old.

The implication of Moses' requests to Pharaoh was that right before the exodus they were not sacrificing in Egypt at all. They knew enough to cry out to God, though, and He came to the rescue.

One thing must be said from the start. Atonement = covering. It does not equal the clever At-One-Ment that many taught in years past trying to simply the concept. They didn't dumb it down, though. They misrepresented it. It is a relationship term, not a status term.

The cross goes **way** beyond this, but this is what kept people going until they got to the cross. They got a taste of what God could do, and also eventually benefit out of it. Hebrews 11:39-40 implies that God grandfathered those of the old covenant into the blessings of the new covenant. It says that they will be made perfect with us who are in Christ. But what if they hadn't been covered? I don't know the answer to that.

Coverage is important. We talk about insurance coverage, paint coverage, cell phone and satellite coverage and having you covered in a gun battle if you're in a Western. In every one of those cases, being covered was to the benefit of the one covered.

They had one day in which to get covered. We currently have more than that to get covered for health insurance under certain programs, but they had one day. If they missed the day, they missed out until next year, and I don't know what kind of a real burden that would have been to have operated under for them. You also have to wonder about the sins that piled up between atonements. What effect did they have if someone died in between? I don't think the Bible tells us about that. It doesn't satisfy our curiosity about what if, but tells us what to... do.

This was like a spiritual April 15th on which things would all get taken care of. Chinese New Year is something like that. One of the elements of it, as traditionally practiced, is to get your books in the black completely. I believe others in ancient days would have understood getting all your accounts settled with God and man at a specific time. They may not have used the right method of this sacrifice, and they may not have acknowledged the right being as God, but the concept of getting your spiritual house in order on one day wouldn't have been foreign to them.

On the contrary, we in the modern era are used to operating on the basis of "revolving" credit in more than the financial realm. I know about this. I worked in an industry where I saw thousands of credit reports.

No one wants to balance the books and bring everything to an end in much of the economic world. Thus, the national debt. My idea would be to compartmentalize all that debt and from now on only spend in one year what came in during that one year. You wouldn't get the debt paid off, but it wouldn't grow, either. But, we can't do that. We have to have more and more even if we're doing it with less and less.

On the spiritual level, for the Christian every day can be in a sense the equivalent of an atonement day, although the New Testament doesn't even use the term atonement. That would lead me to believe that atonement was strictly an Old Testament phenomenon.

The point for us is to get everything that is between us and God out of the way. We do that in I John 1:9, but looking at in principle here we see the power of this. The difference is that in the New Testament it is forgiveness, and we, rather than simply our sins, are forgiven.

The blood made the atonement. (17:11) Blood is opaque. You don't see through it.

Blood always signifies and end when it is shed. Usually, it's the end of the person's life, but here it is the end of their death.

The covering atonement is made for the person needing it. They can't do it for themselves. You can confess, but only God can atone. You cannot atone for anything.

People use the term in popular culture and in old love songs where the two timing lover hopes to atone for what he's done, but they really couldn't do it. No one can atone for the wrong they have done. God has to do the atoning.

The result is that they are cleansed. Only God can do that in both covenants.

One summer I worked in a steel drum factory. I stood at the end of a blast furnace where the drums we were reconditioning were burned out before being washed and repainted and sent on their way. It was about the dirtiest job I ever did. No matter how much I scrubbed and scrubbed, there was still some dirt on the pillow and sheets beyond the norm. Eventually, when I finished that job there was no more of that. My efforts (or maybe just the outer layer of skin finally got rubbed off) got me clean. Atonement is different from that.

The point is that I could eventually get the dirt off. This is something no one could eventually get off by any means of their own or of all the king's horses and all the king's men.

To be 100% cleansed is remarkable. This here is not physical dirt, but moral filth. Sin.

Sin is an act against God in defiance of God. You can't get it off.

Sin is cutting the corners and cutting off others and promoting self. You can't put the corners back on or buy people off. You can't make it so they're not hurt by what you did.

Sin doesn't really leave a good taste in anyone's life. It's not the murders committed by the Macbeths which are satisfying in the play, but rather their downfall and judgment. Even that, though, doesn't bring anybody back. It just balances the books in their lives and gives the nation back to itself.

If you won't let God close the circle by dealing with your sin, you'll get caught as Ahab and Jezebel did. Ahab repented at one point, but he still came to a bad end, and Jezebel. Well, her ending wouldn't be depicted accurately according to scripture in a G rated film.

Sin – the act, the consequences, the guilt, the state it leaves you in – it's all like quicksand. You get deeper and deeper.

The white knight can't touch you. Only Jesus can. To be cleansed is to be pure and capable of approaching God.

You will be clean from **all** your sins. Atonement doesn't pick and choose. It's not like a drug which is not effective in every case. It is effective in every case.

Where you will be clean is before the Lord. He thinks differently than the world does. With them, we can never change our spots.

One of my favorite stories is about El Cid and the cowardly knight. This doesn't appear in the Charlton Heston movie, but it's in the pages of one of the legends somewhere. It seems that one knight was no good and all the others wanted to throw him out, but El Cid said, no, that he would take care of it. He did so by having the fellow sit with him at the dinner table and be with him through the day. Of course, you know what everyone said about that.

The first time the battle alarm rang out the fellow just stayed at the table. Days passed, and the next time it did so, he got up. The third alarm found him going to the edge of the tent where they ate. Each time a cry rang out he would get up, and each time he would go a little farther than he did the last time until finally he was out in the thick of the battle and was the strongest and bravest of them all. What made the difference was having El Cid associate himself with this man, and it rubbed off.

Now, we're not saved because the character of Jesus rubs off on us, but we're saved by being associated with Him, by partaking of every meal with Him, but living in His presence. That takes time. God demonstrates His love and patience in His cleansing. He knows we made our bed, but He doesn't want us to lie in it.

Up to this verse we've had the mechanics of this day of atonement. We had the bull offered for the sins of the high priest. Then there were the goats for the people – one sacrificed and one set loose and what that did for them. What the fellow who released the goat was to do for cleansing of himself after that was set forth very specifically. The point of all that was not to satisfy some regulations and jump through hoops and hoops of red tape. The point of all that was to get to where this verse says they were going to be.

Before the Lord is the place to be. That's where anything can happen.

I stand before my fridge. There are 3 almost empty ice cream cartons in it. Not much there to inspire the heart for very long.

I stand before God. There is everything. He doesn't have assets like a bank; He **is** my asset. He can balance any sheet when He takes care of my sin for me.

Deuteronomy 29:29
15 March 2014

God never says, "That's for me to know and you to find out." If He wants a thing to be unknown, there will be no finding out of it.

The secret things are unrevealed things. They are there, but they're not out in the open. They already exist.

God would not conceal anything from us that would be to our detriment. So, these must be something more to the good and not a snare that will trip us up.

Are they things beyond our power to comprehend?

Are we not yet ready for them?

Are they things that some would misuses?

They are secret. They cannot be found out. That doesn't mean we won't know them, just that **we** won't find them out.

Paul Tournier wrote a little book called <u>Secrets</u> about the power of secrets in our personality development and lives. We grow to an extent when we can control our own inner knowledge and information. Secrets are also a vital element in fellowship when they are shared with the right people. I'm not doing his ideas justice, but you get the idea.

The secret things are probably the gospel truths we know now, but which they didn't know then.

These people needed discipline more than freedom. Freedom changes things, but truth never changes. It is always what it is. Detach the truth from the word of God and imagine the message at the end of a 1500 year game of "Telephone". I don't believe we would have been hearing of Jesus. Maybe, that's what the scribes and Pharisees were giving out, anyway.

Secrets can be difficult. I know someone who once wanted to know all the secrets. Then, when they started having them unloaded on them, they sang another tune. Then, they were glad not to know so many things. Don't think in terms of things kept from us, but as things saved up for us for when we are ready for them and can use them.

God is able to keep a secret and keep it inviolate. By keeping it secret, He could have changed His purpose with regard to Jesus, but He doesn't. The secret is kept intact so that its power may be complete.

God revealed much through the prophets, but the fulness was revealed in the Son. (Hebrews 1:2) This all belongs to God. It is His absolutely. Salvation is not "ours" to create and modify as we will. it always belongs to God.

The Yahweh is, as we have stressed over and over, the only one. Secrets can be lost with people who die. Thus, no one knows about where the pirate treasure is buried or how to find the roads to lost mines.

Since God always is, His secrets are never lost. He always knows where to lay His hands on them. They are safe with Him.

He also knows the proper time to reveal secrets. We have been embarrassed by "speaking out of turn" at times. Not God. The secret is contained in Him.

He is **our** God. We claim Him. We cannot deny Him and hope to have this secret.

A secret is always for an inner circle. It is for those who are a party to it. it is not a solution open to anyone who might care to search it out and discover it. If God had waited, we would still not know the secret.

The things revealed are a different matter. They are out in the open. They are former secrets which have been given to us. By the way, we have more revealed things than we can deal with now.

In the day in which Moses is speaking, though, this would include everything in the first four books of the Bible, plus all that Moses had spoken of Deuteronomy up to this point.

Sometimes we dismiss the Torah as old. Yes, it is part of a previous covenant, but it is profitable as set forth in II Timothy 3:16-17 since it is scripture. But, imagine a time before even these Torah things were known.

The children of Israel in Egypt would have had to rely on oral history. They knew something about creation and their family and God, but remember that Abraham was over 500 years in their past. Without a written record what would we know of Columbus, Cabot, Ponce de Leon, etc? What would we know of the pilgrims and 1776 and everything since up to the beginning of our consciousness of events in our own lifetime? Now, the modern world could not operate without a written record, yet that's what they had to do.

But, as Moses speaks and writes we know that these things are revealed. What did they do with this revelation of what was previously hidden from them? What do we do with a previously hidden revelation?

They were forced to decide. Joshua would force the choice again in Joshua 24. All the prophets from Moses to Jesus forced a decision. The minor prophets in particular were taken up with personal appeals to their readers.

I saw Mt. Hood all the time as a child, but never climbed its peak. I don't think many Portlanders did. Truth cannot be admired from afar as though it were a majestic mountain peak we had no intention of climbing or even photographing and sticking the picture in an album or somewhere on our desk where we'd constantly see it.

Truth must be climbed to the top. We have to plant our flag

there, not to take possession, but to show that we arrived.

These things now belong to us. they are not to be used as we desire, but to be used as intended. Even in our world we have products which are marked "For Intended Use Only".

It's no good clamoring to be admitted to the secrets when you have not yet entered into the revealed things. Revelation is enough in itself, strange as it seems to put it in those terms. A person could own a thousand Bibles, none of which they had ever read. A person could memorize the entire Bible and not enter into it. That's exactly what was done in the episode of the 60s "I Spy" television show entitled "Child Out Of Time". A little girl who had a photographic memory could recite any Bible verse asked for as well as lines from Shakespeare and other sources. The one thing she couldn't do was to pray. I think that was changing by the end of the episode, but it is an extreme kind of illustration of the fact that having or even knowing scripture is not enough. It has to be believed and done.

It's not knowing revelation, but walking in it that matters. We may hesitate to walk in someone else's moccasins, but we should have no reluctance to walk in our own tailor made ones. That's why God gave His law, which was made for man, to man, to walk in it. these are ours that we should know them and do them. these are ours so that we should not be ignorance.

They are not only for us, but for our sons, i.e. the legitimate heirs. At this time that was gender specific. In the new covenant the term is broadened in scope.

God intends that truth should be handed on. It is not to be hoarded. It is not for one generation alone. It is to belong to us forever. We will lose nothing, so we can afford to hand it on.

God does not intend a transitory relationship. It's not one of those camp relationships. There's no going around singing "Friends Forever" (a song which has no relationship to reality) at the top of your lungs and then next year mankind new forever friends because you don't know where last year's are.

We were designed to be a part of eternity,. That is not an add-on to human nature. It is why, if a person does not choose heaven, they choose hell. They are eternal, and if they won't be eternally with God, they will eternally without Him.

The point – observe, do, fulfill. We are not to be Law Looky-Loos, but on-task obedient observers, and by observers I mean ones who fulfill all the laws. I guess I've spoken in almost a circle here, but this is something of a complete circle. This means to do it all, to hold it sacred and separate.

We are to remember what we're separated to as in observing a holiday. So many more people remember to get supplies for their barbecue than they remember the Faithful Dead on Memorial Day.

We are to observe what God has revealed. It's all the words. There's no pick and choose. Nothing is outmoded or passé. We never evolve past the word of God.

It is of this law, of this covenant. In our case, God changed the covenant as cited before the fact in Jeremiah 31 and after the completion of the change in Hebrews 8. But, it is always His covenant which He gives to us.

In the last chapter there were blessings and curses set forth. The whole law must be kept. Even the New Testament is clear on that in James 2:10. God has not changed this in either covenant.

Each covenant is a whole. It requires no completion by man as it has no missing or undeveloped parts. It comes complete from God. It is capable to do all that it says. It challenges us in our entire lives. It is useless if even a piece of it is detached. We are covered or we are exposed. There is no partial covering.

We can have life. Without God giving this to us, we could not.

Faithfulness in revealed things leads to more things being revealed.

Leviticus 26:44
16 February 2019

This doesn't come out of the blue. Get the full context. It's after they confess their iniquity in verse 40.

This is not a Calvinistic type response of God. It's not fiat without anything else in the mix. It comes to those who have repented. God does not forgive without repentance. That's a little sidelight of this, but the point of this verse it that with God repentance works. It's not because of use, but because of God. Without repentance we have no guarantee that God will work for us after we have sinned, only that He will wait until the end to deal with it finally and completely.

Yet is a contradictory word. Whatever comes ahead of it, yet can change it. What comes ahead here is they don't obey God.

What does God do when we do wrong? He waits for us to repent, and He waits until the end.

There are exceptions to God waiting such as in the cases of Nadab and Abihu in the Old Testament and Ananias and Sapphira in the New Testament. In those cases the people who did wrong clearly knew what they were doing before they did it. they didn't make a mistake. One principle coming out of these illustrations is that God is not required to wait. If He waits, it is only because of His goodness in allowing a time to repent, not because such a time is required of Him or part of some kind of contract we have with God.

What happens is in spite of this knowing disobedience. God is not moved by our wrong. he doesn't change the rules to accommodate, but also He doesn't blip us out of existence into dust as the villain of the Avengers "Infinity War" film did.

This takes place when they are in the land of their enemies. In this case it's going to be Babylon, the land of the exile. They were there 70 years. That's more than my lifespan at present. When I was a kid, 20 years was outside my lifespan, both in the past and in the future. They were going to be there, not because of the strength of the enemies, but because of their own sin.

They were enemies because they were against God and because His people were where they wanted to be or because they couldn't stand them. The "gods" of Babylon were not tolerant as D. W. Griffith painted them in his silent epic, "Intolerance". He didn't get Jesus' story right, either. Jesus was not a victim of intolerance, but a deliberate sacrifice to God by God. God rattled Nebuchadnezzar's cage a couple of times, but they were still serving their own gods and abusing God's temple artifacts in Belshazzar's day, just before the kingdom fell.

The enemies would have the people, but God would control the enemies. We say, "Out of sight, out of mind," but we are never out of either with God.

They were under judgment in the midst of the enemies, but God did not want their punishment to end them. One day the judgment which ends all one way or the other will come, but not yet.

God is declaring His faithfulness. He will not do what they do in verse 15 above.

I will not reject them. God won't refuse to hear them or rescue them.

MacArthur said, "I will return," and he did. It was a statement perhaps politically driven and certainly not 100% guaranteeable, even though it worked, but God's statements are totally trustworthy always.

To reject God's statements would be to no longer care for them. It was be to leave them in the foreign lands. We pride ourselves that we will not leave a fallen comrade behind. We honor the body even when the man has left. How much more should we attempt to rescue our people in bondage. When a government does nothing it is a shame to a nation. God will not shame Himself.

God won't abhor or destroy easier. It would be easier to do those things that to redeem. I don't like having "open" items on my books. I like to have "Paid" or "Finis" marked on them. I like to know it's done.

God's patience is what carries people on His books even when He has rejected them in judgment on their sin.

God will not abhor. He will not have a totally violent negative reaction against us. God never says, "I can't stand _____."

He wouldn't destroy them. Exile is terrible and terrifying, but it is not destruction. We want weapons which will destroy the people and leave the property. God destroyed the property and kept the people. To destroy the people He would have to break His covenant. Hell is not breaking the covenant, but to destroy them would have been. Ultimately, the old covenant culminated in the new, and they people who wouldn't make the transfer lost out even on the old or so it seems.

If God had never sent Jesus He would have broken the covenant. God establishes the covenant. We accept or reject it. If we reject, then we are outside the covenant, but as long as we die in it, God will not fail us, no matter what happens to us.

Why? Not because He likes us (though He does), but because He is the Lord (Yahweh) their God. The ground of all God's acts and promises **is** God. That's why we can even have faith.

We are even today, even now in enemy territory. Dealing with the negative giant entities in our lives, though, is not the defining character of our existence. Things don't get easier. God didn't promise that. What He did was better. He sent Jesus.

Jesus two things. He overcame the world. He is with us until the end. That's the same as this.

Numbers 7:89
20 February 2016

This comes after the offerings which are basically the tabernacle start-up. They don't start up the building, but the worship. They are the utensils and the sacrifices.

Building programs, sad to say, have split churches. People who haven't been "on board" have withheld their offerings or jumped ship to another congregation more to their liking. The ship wasn't always sinking when they left, but their departure didn't help to keep anything afloat by the withdrawal of their persons, gifts, and stewardship. There is a building not far from us which was started and not finished for that very reason. It's sad to see it.

People get too attached. I can remember hearing Karl Ketcherside preaching a sermon called "Strangled By Structures" at a revival in our church when I was in high school. It wasn't about church buildings, but about any kind of forms or constructs in the thinking of members of the church which is not from scripture or the Spirit.

This was in place, and it was right. Moses went into the tent of meeting. He was not functioning as High Priest, but as Moses, Mediator between God and Man.

The meeting part of the name of the tent is significant. Meetings are with persons. God is the quintessential archetypical person. He is the center, the whole, not the margin or outside the pale. God is met where **He** is. We have to go there.

The Holy Spirit, in the new covenant, is God where we are. This doesn't preclude going to the meeting place. We do that to show our allegiance to God, to minister to others, to participate in the fellowship, to show the world where we stand.

No one wondered what Moses was doing **there**. Moses went to speak with God.

Why do we go to the meeting house?

Duty?

In a rut?

To impress others?

Anything good at all?

Here's how we really meet God.

In our praises. No one is deaf to praise, certainly not God. this is not because He is an egoist, but because our praise means, "We got it!"

In our prayers. These are to Him alone, not to Darius or anyone else.

In the Lord's supper. Where two or three are, there is Jesus.

In the word,. This is not just an instruction session or a

livelihood for the preacher. It is life for us.

Our meeting God does not depend on our sense of it. We don't know we met God by feelings, but by the changes in our lives. So many say that they are going to change, but so few change, even among Christians or so it seems.

When we have met God we have a corrected outlook. We are more like Him than we were before. What has changed is our thinking, our point of view, our frame of referent. One of the comments that my wife made after I had started to memorize entire books of the Bible (see my book, Ground Work, for explanation of that process) was that I had really changed in significant ways.

If we have troubles or feeling we can't deal with, we have Someone to go to. Like Moses, we can meet God when we meet Jesus. He is not kept at a remove from us by a building or a hierarchy or a sacerdotal system.

With Him there is dialogue. We see the times when Moses "stood up to God" and got a change in God's expressed will. This was not in any way an implication that God was inadequate, but showed that He is open to us. Another example is Hezekiah getting his 15 more years.

God at times gives in, not always because it will be right. Certainly Manasseh born three years after Hezekiah's fifteen year extension was not God's idea, but God does such things for us to show that He is not Immovable or Impassive. He is not a stone idol. He is the Living God who can take into account even our ill advised requests. By the way, I don't know why God gave Hezekiah the extra years and denied me some things that I wanted just as much if not more, but I know He has given me other things.

Meeting. Speaking. The God of all dialogues with us as though we were peers. We can talk to Him.

Moses was in a unique category. He heard the voice speaking from the mercy seat. He may not have been behind the veil, but He knew that's where it came from. If we had been a fly on the tent curtain we'd have heard it, too. It wasn't a vision or hallucination.

This was the mercy seat on the ark. The ark was the place of the covenant. That was fixed. The mercy seat was the place of the present activity of God. it was not a place of precedent, but of providence.

God never made a precedent out of his provision. A prominent example is the bronze serpent which was designed for a one use only application. We do that, though. Something does good one time, and immediately we want it to do it again.

The mercy seat says that every provision of God is fresh, just for us now as we are. It is founded on the covenant, the expressed will of God agreed to by us.

We have in here the testimony of God's will. We're talking about the two tablets. Funny thing about those. I never really thought it before I did this entry, and I don't know that I've ever heard it addressed in any teaching or preaching I've ever heard. The Bible doesn't say specifically what was on them. The usual assumption seems to be the ten commandments, but the none of the texts in Exodus 24:12, 31:18 or 34:1 specify what was on them. It only says that God wrote on the second what had been on the first. I would assume that it is something which we have in the written text we have received, but even then I don't know. Whatever it was, if we needed it, I believe we were given it. God doesn't keep anything secret which we would lose out on by not having it. There's no hidden agenda with God. The point of these was to teach them and make sure people knew them and did them.

The two cherubim were part of the mercy seat. We assume that they were angelic beings of some kind, although we're never given specific information as to their origin or nature or even much about their function. They are great, though, because God rode on the back of one in Psalm 18:10. We have creatures with four faces in Ezekiel one face of which was designated as being the face of a cherub and four living creatures in Revelation which we call cherubim, although they're designated as such. We have taken the cherub part in Ezekiel and applied it to the whole and then taken the similarity or Revelation and applied the cherub designation there as well.

Whatever these are, they're looking out for us and our needs. They're where the blood went on the day of atonement. They would then seem to be connected with covering sin. The living creatures in Revelation praise God for what He has done, and nothing that He has done for man is greater than mercy.

Mercy is not a mere psychological event. It is divine. It is administered by divine beings. It is not a "lucky" chance.

Mercy is God's choice for us. He speaks through His own means to communicate this to us. His speaking is always deliberate. God spoke to Moses then. He will tell us what we need now.

And, He will give it to us.

Exodus 18:11
27 January 2018

This is the testimony of an outsider regarding our God.

Paul said later that elders were to have a good reputation with outsiders in I Timothy 3:7.

Jethro, from what we are told in verse 1, is a Midianite priest. We don't know what or who he is a priest of. I don't think it ever says, but he doesn't seem to be antagonistic. From this verse, though, we see that he's an outsider. Others, such as Nebuchadnezzar and Darius, acknowledged God. It's never recorded that they took the next step of making Yahweh their God, though.

Here, in the next verse, we see that Jethro sacrificed to Yahweh. So, there was some relation.

This is where the light comes on. Now – after all these. He had heard of all that God had done, and in this statement he shows he believes it.

Do we believe what God has done? I mean, we need to believe that **GOD** did it. We need to ascribe to His doing of it. Jethro did.

I know. I didn't know when I wrote the entry the Hebrew word whether it was intrinsic or learned knowledge. It appears, after looking it up in the Analytical Lexicon, to be more of the learned variety. This means that he figured it out and got it. He had taken all the data and made the right conclusion from it. How often do we do that, even about things that we know are right and from God?

Jesus gave miracles, yet people weren't convinced. Jethro didn't see those miracles, but he could say, "I know." When I was in college one of the songs that we sang was a show stopper called "I Know". That was testimony.

There is something empowering in the declaration of the knowledge of God that we have. This isn't an egghead showing off. This is faith. this is the knowledge of believing.

He knew that Yahweh is greater than all the other Gods. This means that he knew something about both.

He names the name here – Yahweh. He gets specific. It's not just Jethro crying "Uncle", confessing that your God can beat up my god, but that your God is greater than all other gods.

Greater is a word of relative worth. He's apparently not ready to say that Yahweh is the one and only indisputable god, but that He is greater than all the others. That is something, but what he needs to say is, "Your God is God." He is who He says He is. I'd like to think that before it was all over, he went all the way. I think he acknowledged Moses for going all the way.

I've worked with non-Christian people who didn't accept God themselves, but who acknowledged my choice and even praised me for it.

Our God is greater, not merely in degree, but complete supremacy. Actually, that was one of the things God demonstrated in the plagues. Every one of those showed His supremacy of some Egyptian god or another. I didn't think that up myself, but got it from a presentation at a convention in the 1980s. Even the magicians said at one point, "This is the finger of God." They may not have thought Yahweh as it's just God in the text, but they knew He was something. Today the world doesn't even do God the courtesy of acknowledging His existence.

God is greater than all the gods. He takes them all down. None can compete with Him to the least degree.

God is personal. He is a person. He trumps every personality. They wouldn't have even been thought of if He had not been Person before them.

Indeed! An exclamation. Is God so old hat to us that we can't exclaim over Him? This is and should be remarkable. We should be the ones doing the remarking.

According to the New American Standard translation it was proven, not just asserted, and Jethro sets it forth in those terms.

We can **hardly** prove conclusively **anything**, either in the courtroom or the laboratory or anywhere else. This is proven to Jethro's satisfaction. All the evidence has been presented and assessed and this conclusion has been arrived at.

The gods did their worst. They dealt proudly. Satan is still doing his worst and doing it proudly. So are all the other evil negative forces in both the spiritual and material realms. The gods didn't "say", "Here we are." They asserted themselves proudly, forcibly. They did not leave God's people alone.

The world may should, "Plurality," and "Don't judge," but we're not included in that plurality. They are a monolithic judging force. Procrustes is the mythological illustration. For those who don't know his grisly story, he had a bed, and everyone had to fit or he'd make them fit by either stretching them out or cutting them down to size. Someone later took care of him in the same way according to the story about him. People do what he did with regard to their ideas, even if they don't do so with regard to physical alterations.

The action is always against. It's adversarial, antagonistic. We shouldn't be surprised that people don't like us. Peter said that in I Peter 4:4. Because we choose Jesus we are almost destined for this.

They are against the people, that is all the nation of Israel.

Egypt had Israel in her power. From a worldly standpoint she could have done what she wanted. She attempted genocide through birth control, but God looked out for His people.]

We are **the** people of God. We are **His** people. He has made one flock of us. He is our shepherd. Jethro doesn't say that her, but we know it is so.

The relationship with God. it is a relationship of putting ourselves under God. To understand that, we have to figure out this first: why would anyone want to do that?

If is suppositional. It's voluntary, not required. God will never make a vow in your name for you. Every relationship with God is freely entered into. Every if your mother "Drug" you to church, as people say when talking about having a drug problem in their childhood, you have to make the decision once you get there. "A Volunteer For Jesus" as we sang when I was a child is not far off.

Why?

Because God made us and knows us.

Because god can get us through.

Because God can fix it.

Because God can be relied on.

Because God knows. He knows what we can do. I keep coming back to the film, "Babette's Feast", in which it was acknowledged that our talents, even if unseen here in earth, and known by God and will delight the angels in heaven. I guess I'd like to see some of that attention now.

If assumes that a person does this. Let's make it personal. It's if I (you can put yourself in the equation) do this.

A man is anyone, inside or outside the covenant. Of course, in essence, coming into the covenant is tantamount to a vow, although in the old covenant they entered involuntarily when born and circumcised into it. Covenant is what God does. We either accept or reject. It would appear that even those in the Old Testament who didn't have a say I the acceptance could reject at a later date.

A vow is another matter. It is a specific binding of ourselves to a specific purpose, practice or time. A vow is not just a promise. It is a sacred promise, an oath of our own life to God.

This is scary because there are no promises given ahead of time on what the vower will get for this. I don't even recall a promise of any kind connected with the specific Nazarite vow in Numbers 6. There, he just dedicated himself to the Lord.

A vow has no compass point other than God. there is no obligation before, but all obligation after. It's voluntary, but you have to consider before you volunteer.

A vow to the Lord. what could this be?

I will only serve you.

I will not sin or do a particular sin.

I will always be in the assembly.

I will pray and read.

I will be like Jesus.

I will treat others like Jesus (either like he would treat them or as if they were Him).

Etc.

All these are things I should be doing anyway if I'm in Christ, but it still takes our commitment to do them.

This is more than a casual arrangement. It is a binding life commitment. It's even more binding than joining the French Foreign Legion. Are we ready to make such a vow. Are we ready to pledge our lives, our fortunes, our sacred honor or would we rather keep those to ourselves?

A person should weight coming to Christ. Even He urged us to count the cost.

The vow is always to the Lord. it's never just floating out there in the air. Yahweh receives this. It's not just another scalp on His belt, but a cherished possession guarded over more carefully than the Mona Lisa is.

Another alternative is to take an oath. An oath sets forth a condition and a consequence. A vow is just the condition.

For example a vow would be, "I give this $5.00 bill to God." an oath would be, "I will give this $5.00 bill to God, and if I do not, I will lose it and more. Both are voluntary. Both are binding.

We might ask, is the oath to anyone, either God or man? could be. In that case, the oath to other people is binding also.

Just because we initiate entrance does not mean that we can initiate departure. This is not a job we apply for and then quit. It's more like a marriage situation only there is no divorce court that can separate us from it.

There is an obligation here. The one who does this has to. This is not a "Much obliged" kind of reactionary response, but a first strike act of relationship.

He shall not violate his word. These are not the pie crust promises someone once spoke of – easily made, easily broken. What is the binding feature is not God's character, but the character of our word. What we say has a permanent, eternal life. That's why coarse jesting is condemned. It's why the teacher is so carefully scrutinized in James 3. what I heard about words being locked up in walls and artifacts once may be only a science fiction talk, but I wonder. Isaac Asimov's time viewing machine in his short story "The Dead Past" proved not to be so dead.

What we say to God is even more inviolate and permanent than anything else we might say in this world. Circumstances may keep us from fulfilling a promise to someone, but God will not accept such an excuse. even ignorance or naiveté is not an excuse.

This is binding. Even the Fonz believed it when he thought he was married though he really wasn't. To do other than we have said is to violate. It is violence.

He shall do this. It's a self-imposed moral imperative. this is why decision making and bed-making can be so perilous. Shall is a word of obligation.

This proceeds out of his mouth. It leaves the person and gods to God. it is verbalized, not merely thought. Although God does know the thoughts and intentions of the heart, it is apparently the saying of it that is binding.

What are we bound to, then? Not only our own word, but to God. our word in a sense becomes His word. Will he let such a word fail, if the fulfillment depends on Him and His Spirit?

NO!!!!!!

That's the value of the voluntary.

Numbers 13:30
23 February 2019

They spied out the land, not to know its strengths, but to know its roads and access points and places to attack. They were looking for what they were wanting to move into rather than even thinking about who they were going to dispossess. The victory was already assured. This was only to be the prelude to that.

That's the basis on which Caleb speaks. He's trying to tell people who don't want to listen what is really to their benefit, but which they are not going to listen to. Despite that, he knows he has to say this.

Caleb did quiet the people. He was to an extent, personally respected. He would survive the 40 years and get a special inheritance in the land.

Sometimes, though, we're like Caleb. We can be in a situation – even in the middle of covenant people – where we are the only voice for God. that's the time to speak up, not shut up. we have to swim upstream despite waterfalls and bears. Caleb stood for God no matter who else stood with Him. he was verbal for God when no one wanted to hear it.

He at least got the situation to where they could listen. These people were before Moses. Why didn't Moses speak up? I'm not criticizing, just wondering.

Caleb had been there. But, people don't always readily believe the testimony of those who have experienced what they have not experienced. The problem is, even if they had experienced it themselves, as the other 10 besides Joshua and Caleb did, they wouldn't believe. They deny the objective to promote the subjective.

It's no wonder people don't believe the testimony of scripture today when the people who were **in** scripture didn't believe it. Caleb was not motivated by whether anyone would believe. He was motivated by what He knew. .

This can be broken down into five elements.
1.   We should
We live in a world which either acknowledges no shoulds or else which acknowledges shoulds which are wrong. should implies not merely obligation, but approved obligation. "I really think you should." That is an imposition.

This is imposed on the people, not because Caleb would impose it, but because God has imposed it. Caleb includes himself. So many would make others do what they would not do themselves.
2.   By all means
This opens it up. ways and means are all open here. This

means not to be half-hearted or lukewarm. This is to accept the imperative. It is to acknowledge it as indispensable. It is to go for it. this means to exhaust every possibility.

If I don't really want to do something I make an attempt or two and give up. This is taking 'em to court. You don't do that unless you mean it. It's serving the papers and going yourself. It's not letting up for even a second.

3.   Go up

They had been planning that, but not doing it. To go takes energy. It means to fight inertia.

Going up takes more energy than going down, but it's also easier. It takes less concentration because your center of gravity is moving up. Think about how much faster you can climb up a long flight of stairs than it takes you to climb down them. In climbing down you have to be so careful to fight against the downpulling of gravity on your own weight which could upset you.

Up is a destination. It is where we are not now. it is where we should be. I once wrote a song about that entitled "Are You Going Up?"

Are you?

4.   And take possession of it

This is shopping to buy and acquire, not looking. It's not ours now, but we can take possession. It is ours by right.

Now, I know they had to kill to do this, but God told them to do it. we should not impose human sensibilities on the commands of God. He has a right to do this.

It is the giving of God which determines this. We cannot take what God has given to someone else. In the end, they will have it, and we will lose it. If God gives it to us, we should take it. We shouldn't leave it under the tree. Possession is the point of being given the girt.

5.   For we will surely overcome it

There are three strong assurances to us. We are the ones to whom this is going to happen.

Will is the word used here. This is going to happen. It's not merely that it should happen, but might or might not take place. Should doesn't enter into this.

Surely tells us that this is without a doubt. It is a sure thing. People say that beforehand about things they know nothing about. God always knows, and when He says what He knows, we know it. we can say "surely" about this. There is no doubt here.

Suspense lives on doubt. Will it or won't it happen. Things we don't think will happen do happen, in real life as well as in suspense films. The happening of the unthinkable makes it even more alarming such as the bomb which blew up a boy and the busload of people he was riding with in Hitchcock's "Sabotage".

There is no doubt. I'm ignorant of the time of His coming, whish is the most significant event in my future, but not in **any** doubt about it occurring.

Caleb's certainty was substantiated 40 years later.

They were going to overcome it. Wars, athletic events, political campaigns – these are great dramatic endeavors which hang in the balance and which require energy in the prosecution of them.

Hope believes in what is in the future. During World War II while it was still going on, America made films like "Wake Island" which not only honored the men who held out there for long and those who died in the resistance of the enemy's program, but making the film was a way of saying that we had confidence enough to fight the war as they had to die in it. Now, that was a worldly matter, and, as it turned out, we won, but not for some time. They didn't really know what was going to happen.

This, too, is not for some time, but we know that we will overcome. Overcome means that the struggle is at an end and we are on top as the victors and we get everything the victor gets – both the title and the prize.

The tragedy in the story in Numbers is that the nation did not listen to this, but they were told it. They had no call to think they would lose. The ten plagues and the exit and everything since then, including passing through the Red Sea, should have told them that.

As I was writing this entry, Great Britain was working on it's Brexit or exit from the European Union. I didn't know if it will or won't happen, but this I know. They got out of Egypt. Knowing that they should have trusted God for everything else He declared He would do. If God gets you out, He will keep you out, and, even better, He will bring you in where He is.

We're standing in the sandals of Caleb speaking the same kinds of things to the same kind of people today. There's still time for us.

Deuteronomy 10:12-13
9 March 2013

This is the Old Testament equivalent of Jesus' two commandments. It is the bare basic framework. Everything in the law would fit under this umbrella.

Verse 12

Now. This is at the present time. It is a consequence.

Our relationship with God is always present tense.

Israel is the whole nation in all its parts. God never makes a covenant with an exclusive few inside a group because everyone who is in the covenant is in the group.

Israel is a winner to begin with. To engage with God is to win. This is not the imagery of warfare, but of contact. Contact always changes us. contact with God will either soften you or harden you. Your choice.

But, we need to understand what we do when we choose.

What does God require of you?

A. Something is required. It's definite. It can be known.

B. The Lord Your God is at the back of this. Yahweh is the I Am. Your God is personal, like a personal trainer or a personal banker or a personal investment counselor, only He's really person.

C. You. The knowledge of god does not leave us in a moral vacuum. Knowledge always brings responsibility.

This is spoken to the covenant people. God requires faith of all people, but these things are for those who have faith. There is a moral minimum standard, but this is beyond that.

1.   To Fear The Lord Your God.

There is an action hear. Fearing is respecting and worshipping. We should start by being in awe of God.

HE SHOULD FILL OUR HORIZON.

He should be the major in our world, not some "standing somewhere in the shadows" being.

God is big whether we want Him to be big or not, but we need to make Him be big in our lives. If God is little in our lives, He can do little for us. Jesus was not able to do many miracles in His home town where they had little faith in Him.

The object of this is the Lord your God. this is the second time He repeats this. There is to be no doubt or confusion about this. We should always see Him as Yahweh our Elohim. This makes Him even more personal and pertinent. To genericize the names of God is to put Him in a box for convenient storage until we need Him, although how could anything we really need ever fit in a convenient box?

2.   To walk in all his ways.

The action is walk. This is the whole round and course of life. It's mobility. To be in hell is to lose mobility.

We are to be in motion morally. Jesus doesn't want armchair Christians. We see that in the parable of the fellow who hid his talent.

In is where we are to walk. In is a definite place. How much is all. There's no picking and choosing, no deciding that something is too hard or that we don't want to do it.

We walk in His ways. God has walked the road ahead of us. Jesus took the point on the cross.

We move from worshipping God – what could become a once a week pastime – to living the God life. This is a definite picking up of the pace.

3.   And love Him.

It's simultaneous. And is something we do while we walk. This is not – he can't walk and chew gum at the same time. we have to walk **and** love.

Love is again an action. There's nothing sedentary about us. Love covers a broad field. It is the motivation for our lives and the pattern of them. How much do I love God? It is an intimidating but necessary question. We have to answer it.

Love is not left up to us define. I John 5:3 tells us that we love when we keep God's commandments. We know if we live God by how we treat others. (I John 4:20)

God is our objective. What we do we do for Him and to Him as per the last part of Matthew 25.

Just passing the test of "Does this show that I love God?" will keep us out of a lot of trouble.

4.   And to serve the Lord your God with all your heart and with all your soul.

We have another addition. There are a lot of ands here. It's not enough to worship and walk and love. Our manner of living is to serve the Lord. We need to adopt a "You rang" mentality. Samuel had to learn that, and we can learn from his learning it.

The person is the Lord your God. That's the third time He's so designated in this passage.

The how is with all. This will be said twice. Nothing is left to us for ourselves.

Your heart is your inner being. Everything that is inside us should do this. Bach showed this when he signed every composition

SDG. (Solo Deo Gloria - Only God (gets or has the) Glory) Not a bad motto for us to put on our t-shirts, mugs, stationary and business cards.

Our soul is our life force. That takes it out of the realm of theory. It is our psyche. The balance must be complete better inner life and outer expression.

Verse 13

5.   And to keep the Lord's commandments and His statutes.

The Ands keep piling up. There is more and more addition. It's not that God is pouring it on like Cinderella's stepsisters poured more and more tasks on her, but that God wants us to realize that relationship with Him needs to involve every aspect of our person. It's to be a complete circle.

There is a verb here which is an infinitive. It is to be infinite, something always done, something characterizing the person doing it. That verb is to keep.

The Lord's (Yahweh's) commandments are what is to be kept. We need to adopt a "Your wish is my command" mentality. We need to be God's genies at His service.

These are propositional imperatives. They are not unknown or mysteries. There's no wondering about what it is that God really wants.

His statutes are added. Statute is another word for law. The statute seems, at least by connotation, to be more permanent law. They appear to be laws beyond the realm of change. They are Yahweh's, so they don't need to change.

We keep these by reading them and then doing them. They are all Yahweh's.

What about them commandments?

These came from God through Moses. Only Moses spoke to God directly. Only He would know all that God had revealed. There's no other source, no other place to go for this.

Today. These don't take effect in two years. But **are** in effect now. They were in effect even before Moses verbalized them. The people hadn't received them, but they were in the position of those in Romans 5:14 who were subject to death even without the presence of the law. Now, though, there's no more ducking or dodging the issue. Today is the day, not of their creation, but of our responsibility to them.

They are for your good. It's not for God's good. It's not even for our neighbor's good like some of our traffic laws. They are for our good.

Obeying God results in life, peace, joy to use. this is not something dreary, but lightening.

The only way to get off the hook before God is to do it His way. This is not because He's a "My way or the highway" guy, but because He made us and He knows what will work in our lives even better than an earthly manufacturer knows his product.

God knows everything that could go wrong and everything that will bring about optimal performance.

God gets the glory, but we get the good. I'd say that's fair.

Numbers 17:5
25 February 2019

There are several things going on in this verse.

God deals with things. We sometimes wonder if He's going to do anything at all. We want God to fix everyone and everything in the world.

– But us.

We want our way rather than God's way. We love the pecking order. We love the pecking order. People will even peck on God and God's man.

People had been challenging the priesthood, but really they had been challenging God. it's always about Him.

God will not be challenged. Over four times as many people as were killed in the twin towers were wiped out in one swoop for challenging God.

To get back to the positive, God has a place for us that is ours, and He wants us there. "All He wants is you; no one else will do." Those words were in the favorite invitation song used by Hal Martin, P. R. man at San Jose Bible College, whenever he was out in the churches. It's not just true as a call, but as a part of how we operate after accepting the call to Christ.

You are not just another one or one of many. That's not pride, but precision of God in knowing and using us. In this case it was Aaron, but we all have our own cases as well.

Now, I'd have dropped Aaron after the calf, but God kept him. It wasn't that Aaron was great, but that God was great. There was going to be an exhibition.

Sometimes I wish God did that in my life. I can remember churches who wrote back to me telling that the pulpit was full (which meant that my candidacy was rejected) who would go on and on saying, "God called so-and-so to our church," and then they would go on to regale him to the skies. I would always say, "If they know who God calls where, why don't they get on the phone and call Congregation X and tell them that Kevin Levellie has been called to be their preacher, and then that congregation would just call me and not even do a trial sermon or a vote." Of course, I don't know what I would have got then, but the presumption in telling others what God had done was irritating when it didn't seem that God was doing anything in my case.

God is the one who established the priesthood. He is the one who chose Aaron and his line. But, people questioned the choice of God. So, God was going to settle it.

Everyone brought a rod. A rod is not attached to a tree. These were probably the ones they'd used for some time. I don't think this was a situation where smoothing was just cut and still had some sap in it.

God was going to demonstrate by breathing life back into what was dead. That's one of His best "tricks".

In this case it was to designate His approval. This rod would sprout.

We could each get a tooth pick and leave it overnight, but I don't think we'd come back and find a pine growing out of one. That's not the way things are in the natural world. God could do that, but it would only happen if He did it. we would have no hope of it occurring any other way. This, in Aaron's case, was a unique event. The world discounts one-time events as unscientific because they are not repeatable, but God does them. For that matter, the world does non-repeatable things all the time. This shows God and us to be unique.

We know from verse 8 that it was Aaron's rod which not only sprouted, but bore almonds overnight. Even trees in nature don't do that. This is a sign beyond nature. But, do we read the signs.

God was going to show His choosing in the matter. He has the right to choose.

Now, we turn a corner in the verse and come to another element in it.

What God is going to do is to lessen the grumbling.

People like to grumble. We so often regard grumbling as floof, but it's serious business to God. Thus, people grumble no matter what God does. The point of this exercise was to end it all.

When we think of grumbling we need to think of a low, hardly discernable Popeye-type muttering. A word or two escapes to give the idea what is being grumbled against, but for the most part it takes place more inside us than it does out in the world. It does more damage to us that it does good for us.

No one else may even understand your grumbling, but God can. That's why He wants to lessen it, not only to get us off His back, but also to get us off everyone else's back and to get us away from a bad influence – ourselves.

The grumbling was heaped on God. It didn't hinder Him, but kept Him from getting to people as He would have liked to get to them because He would have to cut through their attitude which would sometimes shut Him out altogether.

Grumbling creates a crisis. It did so in 16:41. It keeps us from praising God or praying to Him. Grumblers neither ask nor acknowledge.

It appears as though grumbling was a national pastime. It's too bad they didn't treat it worse than I do our national pastime. That's what we call baseball. I haven't been to a game in over 25 years, and even before then I probably didn't make it to more than 10 professional games in my entire lifetime. I never watched baseball on television, either. I'm just not into sports. It's too bad we can't learn to not be into grumbling.

They were grumbling against Moses, but it was really on God. I once read about a professor in one of our Christian colleges who wasn't very well liked. He set up a dartboard with his pictures and had kids in the classroom use it as a target. Then, he took out the darts and pulled off his picture revealing a picture of Jesus underneath full of holes. I did that once in a sermon, and the friends of the grumblers missed the point and left the church over it. I haven't done it since.

We can draw encouragement that whatever we suffer, it's really God's suffering. He knows and cares and takes care.

God wants to clear grumbling out of the way so that His people will not be consumed by it and will then be taking care of business.

Only Aaron could be high priest for the time. Only Jesus is High Priest forever. But, we are all His priests with access to His chambers.

Quit looking at others, and look at Him!

Leviticus 26:40-42
16 February 2012

Verse 40

Confess. Admit. Say the same thing that God says.

God doesn't enforce this, not even in heaven. I believe that when every mouth confesses it will be because the mouth can't help it in God's presence. We have to be the ones doing it.

We try to cover up. We hope no one will discover it. Who can do that before God?

God never excuses sin, But He will forgive it. theirs is a big difference, but we have to acknowledge it.

We need to get back to this, too. Today, People want others to repent of their politics, but not of sins.

There are three ways their sin is set forth in this verse. They're all sin, but just seen in a different light so that the entire wrongness of it will be set out.

1.   Iniquity.

This is unequalness. Their acts do not equal God's goodness or original intentions for man and the world. They don't come up to the perfect righteous standard.

Do our acts weigh in the balance with God's love expended for us? They never will, absolutely, but we should strive for that.

Sin is not equal to God's goodness in making, loving and maintaining us.

We cannot take responsibility for the iniquity of our forefathers, but we can stop accepting it or defending it or hiding behind it. The liberal way of apologizing to a race whose ancestors were mistreated through presidential decrees and cartoon disclaimers is not what we're talking about here.

We are not to condemn them for what they did as though we were their judges. We are simply to acknowledge that it was wrong.

What is wrong is when present people try to repent for dead people. Can't be done. No one can repent for anyone else, either after the fact or before the fact. This is what it should be, an outlook which marks out the course of the past to avoid it in the future.

2.   Unfaithfulness.

This is another definition of sin. It sounds bad, but not as bad as wickedness. It's just not holding fast all the way or having an occasional lapse or two. That's how the world sees it, but that's not how God sees it.

This is not only objectively unequal to the nature of God and

160

our own nature as His creatures, but it is personal unfaithfulness. It is betrayal.

Nothing strikes at the heart like unfaithfulness. For Gage and How to attack the colonies was bad in our view, but it was expected. For our hero of Saratoga to betray us was unforgivable. We have more respect for Benedict Arnold's British handler, Major Andre, than we do for Arnold himself.

This is unfaithfulness against God.

3.   Hostility.

It goes from least active to most active.

Thus, we have the following little chart:

Attitude	Action	Aggression
iniquity	unfaithful	hostility
in us alone	toward God	toward God in declared war

This is an entire orientation against God clear across the spectrum. Iniquity could be indifferent. Hostility cannot.

The choices we make in life show what we think of God.

Verse 41

Hostility comes to us from God, but only after what we have done. This is a case where our hostility always has to come first. God lets us go first even though He wishes we wouldn't go at all.

The specific of this is the exile.

Homelessness is a terrible thing to face. Hopelessness without God is like living in the Twilight Zone in that episode where a girl went into an alternate universe space behind her bed. They brought her out, but this would like being in there and not being able to be brought out.

There is an alternate to hostility in the or here. Again, this depends not on God, but on us. This puts Calvinism out of the picture. It also puts once lost always lost out of court.

The uncircumcised heart is an inner disposition which has deliberately chosen not to come under God's law. This shows that "Total Depravity" as taught in Calvinism is Totally Wrong. These people can make their decision to repent in the state of being uncircumcised or outside the covenant.

Humble is something **they** do. It's that the heart becomes humbled or low. It puts itself under God.

Humble contrasts hostility. The two are mutually exclusive in the spiritual realm. No longer are they fighting God for their own supremacy. In fact, they re-establish faithfulness by what they do.

They make amends. They strive for balance. We cannot buy

our way out of our sin, but when we repent, mental assent isn't enough. It's not the end of the matter. Look at Zacchaeus.

Verse 42

What god will do comes in four parts, climaxin in what He will do with the present people.

1.   Remember my covenant with Jacob.

Remember doesn't mean that God ever forgot at any time before or that He ever forgets, but that He again actively enters into the covenant.

God makes the covenant. Man breaks the covenant. God is off the hook. It is not very convenient for anyone.

But, when we repent, He re-activates it.

This is with Jacob, the last of the three Patriarchs. We work our way backwards. Like a business or legal file using binder clips, the last is on top.

Jacob is the immediate connection to all 12 of the tribes. He was the hard case, the one who sowed wild oats and went off the reservation for a time. He is the example of the man God had to be faithful to. This was done for the sake of His covenant with Abraham.

His covenant is there all the time. It's ready for all comers. It's not lying in a bunk at the stationhouse waiting for an alarm to call it out. It applies to us when we repent and come into it.

2.   Also Isaac.

He is the least exciting of the three Patriarchs, yet he had his moment. He did the same as Abraham by calling his wife his sister. He abandoned for that moment his faith in God and chose to rely on his own ingenuity.

God did not abandon him. God never abandons.

Isaac came back to trust.

3.   Abraham as well.

Here we have the covenant foundation. People speak of covenants plural in dispensationalism that God made with Adam, Noah and maybe others. Those were about specific things with those specific people. Not for whoever might enter into the covenant.

The covenant God made with Abraham was not about something. it was with Abraham as a person. This is the foundation of the covenant with Isaac and Jacob and **US!**

As well tells us that God doesn't just remember the mot recent. He doesn't wonder, "Where are they now?"

The covenant is the basis of God's relationship. We do not have relationship because God "likes" us, but because He agreed to have it with us. it is God's legal agreement which is the base.

4.   And I will remember the land.

We come back to the present.

The land is not just a chunk of real estate. It is part and parcel of the covenant.

We get more than a piece of real estate.

God's faithfulness to maintain what He gave them shows He will do the same for us with regard to eternal life, our resurrection body, our place in heaven.

The land was to be treated right, not for an environmentalist reason, but because it was God's gift given to them.

In 1974 when President Ford was on the campaign trail for congressional candidates, people were upset because it was a new item that the hat given to him in Fresno in the morning (I was there and saw it given) was lost by evening. That was news. (Actually, it's too bad our political news today isn't that innocent.) God expects that we will live in accord with His gifts. He will maintain them. We just have to keep them out in the open at all times where we can see them and use them.

God will bring us to what He has promised. If we have lost or destroyed it, He will restore it. God (better than Pepperidge Farm) remembers!

Numbers 25:12
28 February 2018

Therefore is a result of taking up the cause of god and turning away the wrath of God. obedience does turn away the wrath of God.

Does it pay to take up God's cause? It is negligible?

There are results to every action because every action is a moral action.

I don't think there was any calculation on Phineas' part. He was already of the priestly line. he simply lived up to what he was in God!!!

That'll do it!!!

Moses was God's spokesperson. He was to convey this message.

Balaam presumed to speak for God, and God did "possess" him and speak through him, but that was only to thwart Balak. It wasn't to justify Balaam. The rest of the time Balaam was no good.

Moses was God's regular spokesperson. Instead of a drawing of the white house behind him, he had the pillar of cloud and the pillar of fire behind him.

Priests made pronouncements for God as did the later prophets, but none of them was like Moses until Jesus who surpassed him. Moses himself had predicted that.

Moses never got into trouble when he spoke God's word. His sin which kept him out of the promised land was adding to it.

He said that this was something to behold, meaning that it was something remarkable. Earlier in the morning when this entry was originally made the fellows around the table were talking about nothing taking God by surprise. That's true, yet it doesn't mean that God doesn't find some things remarkable. (Actually, I think He'd like to remark about everything about us.) He does.

Jesus found faith remarkable. Here, it's acting for God.

Phineas was also a propitiator, turning away the wrath by killing two people. You can only do that if you **know** it's God's will. There were, of course, other God authorized wars and killings in the Old Testament, but we don't see anything of that in the New Testament.

God needs to be satisfied, not because He is "Full Of Himself," but because He is God. it doesn't damage God when we don't do it, but it damages us. It's like an Orson Welles television show I saw in the 70s where someone tried to slash at a painting on a hard surface only to have the knife skitter off and kill themselves with it.

Phineas satisfied God, and now God directs Moses to tell him what he got for it.

God says, "I give." He does this. Yahweh does this. God never loans. He gives. What a God that He can trust us outright with things.

There are very few people I would even loan my 1937 Stamps-Baxter song book autographed by all the pre-plane crash personnel of the Blackwood Brothers, let alone give it to them.

God gives things we would even loan or rent out. Phineas got this for the line of priests. Unfortunately, the line deteriorated in the cases of Annas and Caiaphas, but until 70 A. D. God never took the priesthood away from this line. It went from one branch to another at least once in the case of Eli, but they were still in the line.

Phineas, by the way, was a grandson. He possibly could have seen the golden calf incident and learned from it.

Our grandchildren are watching up. What will they learn from what they see?

The covenant is always God's covenant. That's why He speaks of it as, "My covenant." We enter into it or not, but it is His all the way through. We are never in control of the covenant. God sets forth the conditions and the rewards. Here there don't seem to be any subsequent conditions, but there is a reward – peace.

Peace is what some of the sacrifices were aimed at or what they were celebrating. Peace with God (Romans 5:1) is the goal. Phineas has not peace for the moment, but a covenant of peace. Peace is assured and settled for him. it is not destroyed or upset by conditions around him.

Peace is a stronghold. It is an island fortress in the middle of a raging sea. It is an impregnable city which cannot be successfully breached by siege and which is eternally supplied so that no provision can be cut off.

This is remarkable because everyone else had to wonder about their relationship with God. They didn't know what they were going to get.

Would it be accepted or not, what they were giving to God. in the time of Cain there doesn't appear to have been an expressed criteria, although God still legitimately held Cain accountable. With the law everyone would know the basis of peace with God, but how many achieved it?

The Old Testament is a record of turmoil and betrayal, of covenant breaking on a wholesale basis. God had to resort to the nations to judge and correct Israel at times. he even told prophets such as Habakkuk that that was exactly what He was doing.

So, to have a covenant of peace would be remarkable. It comes to the priestly line.

We are priests to our God, and we get this covenant of peace from Jesus. (John 14:27)

Peace is a fruit of the Spirit. Peacemakers receive a blessing from God. Peace is a greeting in almost every letter. Even the Galatians get it, although there was no thanks expressed in their case.

Peace is not absence of war, but victory unaffected by conflict. When we have the peace, we cannot be overthrown. We should not be disturbed.

Peace is always personal. It comes from the Lord of Peace. (II Thessalonians 3:16)

The covenant of Phineas was described as perpetual priesthood in the next verse. There is went to the descendents. We want our descendents to have it, but in Jesus it is ours eternally because it is not ended with the end of this life. God's covenants have no sunset clauses from His side. They can be broken by us, as is set forth in **both** testaments, but they will never be broken by God. When Romans 11:29 says that the gifts and callings of God are irrevocable it means by Him, not by us, since they are spoken of in their character as coming from Him as the initiator.

God does not change His mind about these things. That doesn't mean that He has not made provision for us changing our minds. Covenants are always conditional.

First condition: acceptance of them. The terms, the terms are set forth and accepted and built upon.

Second condition: continuing in them.

God is not going to keep us on as in a Tennessee Williams or Edward Albee play where people stay socially chained together to torment one another.

Covenants are conditional, but they are also secure. They are not like a warranty which has not expired on a product manufactured by a company which no longer exists. I Am is always back of the covenant. **That** is the bond of assurance. That is the greatness of the covenant. That is why it is peace and not something less.

There is nothing temporary in what God gives. It is designed for eternity.

Deuteronomy 10:20
9 and 16 March 2019

What we are to do.

The same still applies to us in the new covenant. This is in the context of deal with the aliens or how we are to deal with people in the world who are not God's people. We deal with them on the basis of this moral fabric. This is the foundation of all object.

There are four things – four acts and three shalls.

This is a shall corporation. We are constrained and motivated by the shall. We can, of course, refuse it, but it's still what we are supposed to do.

The emphasis is in what we're supposed to do, not what we're not supposed to do. The legalists have gotten it all wrong. No one is saved by not doing a list of sins because before they've ever received that list of sins they've already done enough to need to be saved. You could list everything **not** to do, but that wouldn't mean you did the shalls.

Everyone there is a you. This is universally binding on those in the covenant.

1.   Fear the Lord your God.

The first commandment.

We are specific here in the covenant. Only Yahweh gets this.

In speaking of fear we start with respect. It is focus, attention, all eyes on God. We respect Him for who He is.

The world has no respect for God. Without that you don't need to do anything else. Maybe that's why they're not interested. They don't want to have to do anything. You don't need to do morals without respect for God. You don't need to respect anyone else, either. People who don't respect others only have one standard in their lives – their own comfort. That's how Jesus put it in the parable of the unjust judge in Luke 18.

The insatiable thirst for respect by the world is a thirst for being God. if we respect God, we can respect others, and we will receive the respect we need. But you have to start with who you respect.

Respect always acknowledges that which is larger than us. when we do it to other people, we're not acknowledging that they are greater, but that they are respected because of greater concerns which are not affected by anything they do or can do.

God didn't have to send Jesus to be feared. He got that by being God. when we fear God, we have no time to disparage anyone else.

They needed to come to God alone. He is feared as God – the sole object of worship, the sole power, the sole creator. God shares none of these things with others.

When we bow to Him we don't bend our back, but we humble our heart. All pride is out the door.

2.   Serve Him.

This involves worship, sacrifices, alms, good deeds. Jesus' parable broadened the definition of serving God to include that latter.

We think of doing our duty or earning our points or doing our job, but we need to see it as serving God. If I do something good for you, I feel good, but if I do something for God, I move beyond feeling. I move to communion.

God is the only being who absorbs those who serve, who raises rather than diminishes them. we know this from Jesus' washing the feet.

The servant is the official one. He is the accomplishing one. He works to the end of another – in this case it's the Lord. What end are we working to?

3.   Cling to Him.

A disciple is a learner, but he is also an adherent.

Clinging is the condition. If you don't cling, you fall off. You have to learn how to do it in the right way. I hate it when cling wrap clings to itself rather than to the container I'm trying to use it on. We need to cling to God, not to ourselves.

God will never let go of us, so we can cling with safety. He will never fall and take us down to disaster with Him. He will only go up to the summit and to the victory.

We cling for ourselves so we won't lose out. in the act of clinging we do not get rigid and cramped, but we get conformed to the image of His son. This is getting as close to God as we can get. This takes it out of the realm of duty religion.

This isn't three times a year and only the necessary sacrifices. We're not attracted to people who barely do enough. I don't think God is, either, although it's not always our accomplishments which count with Him as much as it is our endeavors, regardless of how they turn out.

4.   You shall swear by His name.

This isn't the inappropriate swearing that Jesus (Matthew 5:33-37) and James (5:12) both spoke against. This is living a life "By God," rather than speaking that way. You can say anything, but what you do is the real thing about you. We are to live a life that can be lived in truth before God. it's one that is in accord.

To swear by the Lord means that He is the absolute measure of our truth, morals, ethics and standards.

The people were never intended to get an inoculation of righteousness and then go their own way. Swearing by His name – all that He is – only works if you live by His name. Words and works need to be synonymous.

Moses calls the people to a higher standard. It's based in God. You can only swear by His name if you speak the truth. You can only speak the truth if you know the truth. We know Him, and He has set us free.

Moses gives more about God in the next verse. That's necessary because only those who know God can do these four things. We can't expect the world to know or do them.

Exodus 30:29
1 February 2020

This is the establishment of holiness in the world of men.

Holiness is not only for heaven.

Also, it's not inaccessible for us.

These three points must be kept in mind in looking at this verse.

You shall also consecrate them. This is in addition to the anointing of verse 26. It's not enough to just "tap" something, showing that you know it's there. You have to "do" it.

To consecrate is to devote them to something.

Everyone is devoted to something. My wife, Jeanette, once wrote a book (never published) which she called, <u>Devoted To Me</u>. It was all about how her cat Obie showed that he was devoted to her by doing what he wanted to do and ignoring her wishes altogether. Now, it was intended to be a children's book, but it was very subtle in giving out that message.

We show **who** we are devoted to by what we do.

Most people, when they say, "Devoted to me...", they mean themselves. They're not devoted to anyone else.

Our things out to be for God, not for us. sometimes people dedicate a car or a home or a child. That alone won't do it. You can't dedicate your car to the Lord and then use it as a getaway car from a robbery. You can't dedicate and then go nowhere for Jesus in it.

Sometimes people think that as long as they don't do bad, they're O. K., but not doing god is also a way to be un-O. K.

What was anointed and consecrated was set forth in verses 26-28. it included the tent of meeting, the ark, the table, the utensils, the lampstand, their utensils, the altar of incense, the altar of burn offering and its utensils, and the laver and its stand. Everything connected with and contained in and a part of the tabernacle was consecrated. This whole ensemble of things was a way to meet God. That was the end of the things and their reason for being.

God can be met in and through anything we have. This is more than the church building for us, although it should be so consecrated. We are the temple of the Holy Spirit, so everything connected with us fits. It's the same in heaven where the tabernacle there is equated with those who dwell in heaven in Revelation 13:6. This is one thing we will continue to be there that we are here.

Heaven is a place consecrated to God. nothing and no one not so consecrated will be there.

This is done that they may be most holy. Holiness is accessible.

What we do makes things holy. Chew on that a while.

170

I said recently that I have never felt like a person of power. Someone else told me that it was otherwise.

We consecrate everything to one side or the other - God or Satan. Those are the only two sides there are.

Nothing in the universe belongs to no one. The earth is the Lord's. That covers it all here, and no one can make claim to the stars, even though you can pay to have one named after you.

The point is to make these things set apart and different. Anyone can sit down in a chair in the coffee shop that our journaling group meets at. If someone got there before us some Saturday, we couldn't make them move. We might not like it, but we would have to go elsewhere to another table. God will not go elsewhere other than to what is or should be His. If we don't consecrate it, He will take it our of our hands if it's His.

Jesus did not allow moneychanging and livestock sales in His Father's house. it was not to be for that.

This is to be most holy. It's not that some things can be Middle Of The Road Holy or sub-holy, but everything connected with God is to have the superlative about it.

It's supposed to be the holy in use, not in display. Years ago we started collecting Madonna Inn goblets. These are very beautiful rose pattern distinctly colored goblets. For a long time, we just left them on the shelf and only used them if someone really special was over. That meant they didn't even get used once a year. Then, one day it came to me that we should use them more often and not just let them be on the shelf. Yes, we use them for holiday meals or eating ice cream or fruit out of, but their beauty is now not for outsiders, but for us. Yes, they are put in danger in use, but they are allowed to shine as they should in use. God doesn't expect to be put in a closet as with the talent in the parable.

He is set apart so He can be set forth.

Holiness is to be on earth. The secular realm is really the sacred realm. It's not secular by nature. God has to be forced out of it to create the secular, but He won't stay out.

Heaven is not something we only wait for. God gives us heaven to go to heaven in. That's a phrase from a song by Dwayne Friend. I didn't understand it at the time when the song came out, but I do now. He was saying that heaven begins now, not just after the trumpet sound. God gives us heaven by giving us the things of heaven - love, forgiveness, mercy, power, the Holy Spirit.

Whatever touches these things was going to be holy. In Haggai 2:12-13 we are told that holiness is not communicable the way defilement is. That is true of many things, but here it is taking the perfect commonplace, the sacrificial animal without a blemish, and putting it on the altar where it becomes holy and dedicated to God. Before it is put on the altar or in the tabernacle system, it's just meat. By putting it in the consecrated place, it's give to God.

We are never lessened by what we give to God. we have the "More Blessed To Give" pronouncement of Jesus. We have the testimony of scripture that God fills needs. We have the promise of Jesus that He is with us always.

We understand the power of that last statement by looking at went before it. Here is a short list of the difference that Jesus being there made:

- ❖ 12 baskets
- ❖ 7 baskets
- ❖ Safety in the storm
- ❖ Healings
- ❖ Life from the dead
- ❖ Knowledge of God's will we'd have had no other way.

Jesus is with us here today. He knows our needs, but when we pray, he knows that we want Him to do something about them. He knows that we know that He knows.

Do you want to be holy? Get on the altar. (Romans 12:1) no one but God can transmit holiness. Only the blood of Jesus (not that of bulls and goats) can communicate this to us. That blood is so strong that rather than it being contaminated by our sin, we are cleansed.

Whatever. Let's go back to that word. It's unconditional without exclusions. We are included in whatever.

We see our shortcomings.

All God sees is our coming to Him through Jesus. That coming supersedes our shortcomings.

This is all together the power of holiness.

Deuteronomy 5:24
7 March 2020

This is the aftermath of hearing the ten. Moses is telling them what they did and what they got. Actually, he's reminding them what they said. We often need that. we forget our own statements awfully quickly at times.

This is what they saw, heard and realized. They used their senses and came to a conclusion from their experience which was, in this case, the right conclusion. People don't always interpret their own experience aright. We need to get the same things – the information from God and the life beyond the time of getting that to live it.

Behold is a verbal drum roll and bugle call to arms all rolled into one. It is now attention center stage, leaving everything else out of consideration. We're not to see or hear anything but God when it comes to taking direction for our lives.

1.   The Yahweh our Elohim.

There's never any doubt as to who did this and who He was.

They mentioned God by name. They didn't regard Him as the first cause or the prime mover or any other euphemism which reduced God to a force or an impersonal factor. It was the name God used for Himself. They named God. They owned God. They weren't like parents saying to one another, "Your son did that."

It is our. This is a common relationship. I can talk with only two people about "our" mother. No one else fits in that circle. The circle gets wider when we speak about "our" neighborhood or city or country or church. God wants this "our" to have the widest possible breadth. This "our" should be shared by people at Nevins Christian Church, in the United States, in the world, in the totality of all that has been made. (By that latter I don't mean aliens, but Saints who have passed through the gate of death into another realm.)

He is our God, to be worshipped and obeyed by us. Everyone is God's person because He made them all, but not everyone acknowledges the God who made them. They so often bring in a ringer or act as if they found their own way out of the cabbage patch without any help or as if they were a product of existence by spontaneous combustion.

God showed them two things. One is more than enough since no one could do either of them. Two is impossible for anyone but God.

Sometimes glory and greatness are exclusive. We have had celebrities full of a kind of glory, but not great. I particularly think of Mrs. Miller from the 60s. we have great people who aren't known at all. I would classify all of those in my book Contributors in that category.

There are 100 individuals or sets or groups of individuals listed there, and there more that didn't get in the book, not because they were no good, but because I had arbitrarily decided to limit it to 100 when I first went to write it. I'm thinking I may expand it some day and even include the entries I wrote of the legacies of public figures I saw in person who I did not know personally. Some of them, I didn't even remember their names when I came to write of them, but I remembered their contributions to my life.

God has both glory and greatness all the way. He has the fame, renown and light of glory and the mega-ness of greatness. Unlike a mega mall (Between two visits to Olathe, Kansas probably about 4 months apart a few years ago, an entire mall was torn down and even the parking lot eradicated, and it had already grown back to grass. That kind of greatness is subject to change. God's is not.

God displayed glory in the display on Mt. Sinai. He demonstrated greatness in the care of the people, the manna and everything mentioned in Deuteronomy 8, the law given to them for guidance and life, the forgiveness of sins through the sacrifices, the bringing them out of Egypt.

Great beat's Tony the Tiger's comment. God is not merely better than others, but objectively great in and of Himself. Some people say, "I'll show you," and then they don't. God says and does what He says.

2.   We have heard His voice from the midst of the fire.

They had heard it, actually heard it. they didn't imagine it. they didn't only hear part of it or think they heard one word for another. This was God's voice, God expressing Himself. They actually heard this. They didn't imagine it.

The voice came from the midst of the fire. (Exodus 19:18) Normally, fire consumes and draws in. Here, the voice came out. Something foreign to the fire was in the fire. It was not a part of the fire. That's the greatness of God. he can get in anywhere and speak out of anything. In Jesus, God spoke in our midst and in the midst of the flesh of Jesus.

3.   They saw – experienced – that God speaks with man and man continues to live.

In the Old Testament they seemed to have the idea that to see an angel was the prelude to dying. Not so. I don't remember anyone who saw an angel who died from seeing the angel. One angel killed 185,000 in one night, but I don't think it came from them seeing him and then keeling over like people turned to stone in seeing the gorgon of myth.

God is there. God speaks. Those two things are so simple, yet they are such a revelation.

The scriptures are the record of God speaking with man. The Spirit still guides through the still small voice at times. We are given what we need then, though it doesn't count as revelation for anyone else.

God tells us what we would not know otherwise, what we need for salvation, much of what is coming. He doesn't tell us everything we might desire, but He doesn't leave us in the dark. The word is a lamp. God is light. They're the same nature. Illumination is the result to us. By that we can live.

Not listening to God means that we will die.

Deuteronomy 26:18
14 March 2015
14 March 2020

Have you ever wondered about what God thinks about you.

What we are is what God has declared us to be. God has affirmed this of his own free will and initiative. We are certified creatures. These things are even more in the new covenant with regard to those who are in Jesus.

The Lord has today declared this. God is about what is right now. He operates in eternity, but He knows that our need is always for this instant.

In verse 16 He commanded. Here He declares. In verse 16 He commanded that they should do. In verse 17 they declared that they would. To command and to obey lead to the declaration of this verse. We have to commit to obey what was commanded.

I once read a document written sometime in the late 1800s, I believe it was, by a fellow who said that the United States Constitution was not binding on anyone because no one then alive had been alive when it had been framed and ratified, so they were not liable to it. No matter how much that sounds like something you could stand on, you couldn't. It might sound logical, and, to some, even appear as a way to get out of obeying the law, but to follow that line of reasoning, no law would ever be in force for the people born after its adoption. What a legal mess that would be.

If we can't invoke that principle on the constitution, how much less can we invoke it on God? We didn't make the covenant; God did. That's why.

The Lord has done this today. This is done in response to what the people had said that very day. There is no lapse between faith and commitment. You don't have so long to back out of the deal without any penalty. Not making the deal at all is a penalty in this case. Backing out is worse than never having come in at all. (II Peter 2:21-22)

This is current. The word of God is always current. It's always the word of today.

This is now God's response. This does not come until AFTER God makes the offer and man accepts it. In other words, no one can be in without belief. You can't be in because of heredity or heritage, physical or cultural.

You need to take everything back to the source or authority behind it. You have to establish that that authority is legal or legitimate with regard to what you are being asked to do. Yahweh is the declarer. He has declared. He has already done it.

We live in a world of suspense for what someone is going to do. God takes the suspense out of it. Unlike the classic courtroom drama films such as "Witness For The Prosecution" or "12 Angry Men" or "Anatomy Of A Murder", there is no suspense involved. We know our judgment ahead of time because God **declared**.

A declaration is a legal statement which a declarer stands behind. God stands behind this. That's what gives it its power and force. This declaration spells it all out without any gray areas. There are no loopholes.

You're in or out based on what **You** do about what **God** has said. It was that way from Genesis 3 on.

He has declared **You** to be **His** people. That is definitely a unique statement. In the history of "religion" people choose their own God or their own church rules and structure, but here God chose a people.

We are Yahweh's people. We don't just belong to God. Buttoning up our overcoat is not enough. We need to act like it.

We are His people, identified with him and flowing from Him. We constitute a people, that is a unified single homogeneous group. This is not on the basis of culture or preference, but on the basis of blood. For Christians it's the blood of Jesus. For Israel it was the blood of the Passover lambs which created a nation where before there had just been a collection of families.

God calls us His. This is not so He can control or contain, but so He can promote. God's promoting His children is one of the things that God is about. The nation forgot that when they believed the report of the ten.

Some of them acted in such a way that they opted themselves out of his choosing, but He chose. In the Old covenant you could not get in any other way. There were some naturalization clauses in the law, but they weren't doing an Ellis Island business ever.

You = Israel. This is the chain of Abraham to Isaac to Jacob (bypassing Esau) to the twelve tribes.

God now wants all men everywhere to repent, but then the covenant was limited. We are definitely better off.

His people is an inclusive term. People always like teams or countries to root for. The Romans had an entire system based on 4 colors for rooting at the coliseum and the games. Even the emperor would pick a color.

God picks us for His color team. He roots for us. We play for Him. That's because we're His people – a specific identified group, a cohesive body with specific characteristics.

We are to be known to be **His** by our character and acts and allegiance.

God wants us to be ALL His always. This means we in turn are faithful only to Him.

The glue that holds the people together is belief. Belief is a common possession. It's not peculiar to any one group or sub-group. We have no right to keep anyone from it who genuinely wants to come into it. Of course, I am speaking from a new covenant standpoint.

Some countries allow dual citizenship. I had a friend once who was born in the United States, but he had dual citizenship in Switzerland through his father. I don't know what the situation on such things is now in regard to Swiss citizens, but I do not that God does not allow dual citizenship. If we're not citizens of heaven alone, we're not citizens of heaven. We live in the world, but not as true citizens of the world.

We are God's people because God said so, not because we thought so or someone put together a "Let's Be God's People" initiative. This is not a bumper sticker relationship as in some of the faith campaigns of the 70s.

We are a treasured possession.

We all have those, things we are not likely to give away and which we keep a close watch on. For me it would be (thinking in terms of "things" existing in this world only at the moment and not of people or of my Bibles) the Blackwood Brothers song book signed by all of them in the 1940s, other signed books and the beloved books I have read and reread and my music. Out of that group the song book would be #1. For God, we are #1.

He owns the cattle on a thousand hills, all the stars, all the angels, but for Himself, we are #1.

We are treasured. God is determined to hold on to us. He means to keep us and protect us and look at us and delight in us and admire us.

Do you want to be admired by God? Faith will do it. Jesus always marveled at faith, and He always wanted it.

This all is as promised. God said we would be people and possession. Yet, some act as if God really didn't want anything to do with us or as if we were so far below Him that He wouldn't noticed us. Even the Psalmist asked the question: "What is man?"

God's promises are absolute. (Hebrews 6:13-20) All will be as He promised.

Things are not always as I promise. Circumstances get in. I think better of it. I realize that the promise was really wrong.

Circumstances don't affect God. He doesn't think better of it. It was right to begin with. I know we have Genesis 6:6, but that is not reneging on a promise. It is an act rooted in the creation right of God.

What kind of people are we? Slaves? Drudges? Economic units? Cogs? Throw-aways? No. We are a treasured possession.

We all have one or two things that fit that classification. Others may not "see" it, but it's there. We may not even see the value in ourselves, but God does. He sees us as treasure. We are His treasure on earth, just as we have treasure in heaven.

We know our treasured status because of the promise. Hebrews 6 tells us that it is impossible for god to lie. So, when He promises it will not be other than what was said. Omniscience and omnipotence enable the promise to be fulfilled.

God said He would make something of us. A nation. A people in a place of security and provision. These people who heard this were not the ones who had come out of Egypt. The men, other than Joshua and Caleb, hadn't even been circumcised. God was not going to let that omission bring the covenant to an end. His promise is what carried it forward.

That was God's part.

Now, our part.

You – the treasured people.

Should – an obligation, something which is right to do. you can choose not to, but when you choose that you choose damnation.

Keep – obey. We keep by doing, not by storing away or protecting.

All – there is no pick and choose. We like to do what we like to do. we rebel against having to clean our plate, especially if there is sauerkraut on it.

All is so daunting. I'm a completist, but I always find there's another recording or book I have to get in order to be **complete**. I'm starting to give it up on some things. We can't give this up.

His commandments are the express words of God. There is no doubt about God's wishes. We know what to do.

Most of the promises of God are conditional. That doesn't keep them from being promises, but it will keep us from missing out by ignoring the conditions. The promise always depends all the way on God. The getting of the promise always depends all the way on us in terms of our receiving it or rejecting it by having faith or not having faith.

God's gifts once given and His callings once sent forth are not conditional (Romans 11:29). He won't take a gift back because He doesn't want someone to have it, and He won't uncall someone by cancelling the gospel in their case. But, if we reject the gift or abandon the calling, we're out, and rightly so. In that case it's all on us, and none of it is on God. He never puts anyone out who has once come in. They put themselves out. He merely judges them for going out when they should have stayed.

This is on you, not on God. You should keep all His commandments. The people said they would in verse 17, so there's no surprise here.

It's all, not just some. The whole law is mentioned in James 2:10. That has to be it. But, we can do that. Romans 13:10 says so. So, don't despair.

These are not just general guidelines or God's wish list, but what we are supposed to do. If we don't do it, we are failing in what we said. The commandment really makes it easy. We don't have to wonder what God wants.

The ten are not really all that burdensome. Keep away from other gods, do the Sabbath, don't do the major crimes. Now not coveting, the tail end, is a little harder because we all like to do some window shopping, but it could be done. The others are numerous, but they are not difficult. God did not make the law difficult beyond our ability. It is something we can do as it came from God, not as the Pharisees later embellished it.

These are His ideas. We are not to be like Citizen Kane's second wife who gloried in the fact that what she did wasn't his idea. (That's not to excuse Kane – he was wrong – but to illustrate the concept.)

If we love God, we will keep His commandments. Since God has made us His people we can do it.

We quit something because we feel incapable or overwhelmed. The world overwhelms.

God expects a lot, but He helps us every way, especially in the new covenant. So many times we need on word to obey. If Achan had said it to himself, he, his family and 36 men would not have died. That's a terrible price to pay for not saying, "No," to sin.

When we say, "Yes," to Jesus, it will be easier to say, "No," to sin. because we are God's people we can do God's commandments.

Deuteronomy 26:19
18 March 2020

This adds on to the previous verse. There are two more things promised to the people. Whenever God promises something, there's no doubt that it's coming. I've ordered things in the mail that never came. Sometimes there was no explanation. One time a company went totally out of business and I had no recourse or way to get either what I had ordered or the money that I had sent. God sends what He says.

God is going to exalt His people above all other peoples in praise and name and honor. That's a mouthful, and God said it, and we can get it.

God will make His people be on high. Having the high ground is always essential in battle. It's also valuable in terms of living above it all. We experienced heavy flooding in our area over ten years ago. Because we were in a home that was a little elevated above the surrounding fields, and because those fields had adequate drainage, we weren't affected by the floods other than a little bit of moisture that came in the basement. There were people in town who had a couple of feet of water in their basements.

The nation was not just going to be higher than others, although Jerusalem where the capital would one day be was far in excess of elevation over the rest of the land, but it was their position among the nations that was spoken of here.

There is a pecking order, not only in social settings, but also in international relationships. Some nations have more of a voice than others at the world table because of their size, prestige, power or resources. God was going to make His nation such a nation. In a sense they were during the days of David and Solomon politically, but the real way God would exalt the nation would be spiritually through their relationship with Him and the sending of His Son, Jesus Christ.

To be high above all nations may not be to be in control of any of them, but to be better than them. God's people are supposed to be better than the world, not in a prideful way, but in a spiritual way. We are supposed to be closer to the measure of the stature of Jesus Christ. When we are faithful to God, this is where He puts us.

The nations, by the way, think that they made themselves, but God made them. Not ever nation comes into being the same way. Some are created by family relationships or geographic features or by common culture. On the other hand you have the Basque people who have a common culture, but it's spread over a couple of different nations. Nations aren't always defined by colors on the map. No matter how any of them began, God is ultimately the one responsible for making them.

This doesn't mean that everything they do has His approval, but that just as He made everything in the universe, He also made the groupings possible. Rights are rooted, not in political power, but in God.

God made the nations, but through their own free will they abandoned Him to serve other gods. This has always been happening, at least as far back as the time of Noah, and probably before as I don't imagine God just got peeved because one person worshipped an idol the night before He told Noah it was all going to go. Certainly Babel shows this. God made nations there by confusing the languages which, as a natural consequence scattered the people into separate places.

No, God is not a stranger to this world. He knows full well what's going on there. Sometimes, even Christians pigeonhole Him in the "Spiritual Only" category, but there is nothing outside the category God operates in. He is willing to exert His power for us where we are. Moses and the people had just left the most powerful nation in the world. They had seen that God was stronger than Pharaoh and all of Pharaoh's magicians and army.

First, God would make them high in praise. There are some nations that are praised and others that are condemned. It's been that way throughout history and has been so throughout my lifetime and is so today. The praise that comes to the nation is not from the peoples of the earth. Their acclaim is like a mist. It disappears faster than it appears. They often do praise God's people, but they make no move to become part of them, and if you praise someone you'll want to be a part of it. If I said that Bach was the greatest composer who had ever lived, but never bought any Bach recordings or listened to any Bach pieces on the radio or the internet, you'd really have to seriously wonder if I believed what I said. I suppose someone might say such a thing, but not have the money to pursue it, but you would know full well if such an opportunity came their way which they could afford or which happened at a time when they could hear it, and they didn't do anything about it.

What is there to praise in us? That we are in the covenant, for one thing. To be there means that we know God. We have repented. We have received Jesus and are in Him. Our relationship is the totality of what we have as a grounds for praise.

Next, He would give them a name above others. The name is not merely an identifier, but also a reputation. When people say my name, they know who I am, but at present, until I get that "Well done," a lot of people have nothing else that they know to say about me. They can talk about my preaching and my music and my Christmas poems, but in the world at large, that's a small reputation.

God wants to give His people a large reputation. That is the reputation they have before Him and not any other. You could be known by name by every person who ever lived during your life time, but it would be nothing to God knowing your name. His knowledge is the source of our reputation.

Third, God was going to give them honor above others. He caused Israel to be honored among the nations in instances such as the queen of Sheba's visit to Solomon, and Babylon's coming to see Hezekiah when he was in recovery. (He acted wrongly there, but, still, they did come to see him.) Being part of the Israel of God is a high honor.

I can remember how it was when I in high school. Because I didn't do well on the math and science courses, I never got offered a membership in the National Honor Society. When I was a junior, they had an honors assembly toward the end of the year, and in the middle of it all my name was read out for having the French honors. I hadn't been aware that I had taken that. It was given to the highest score in each school participating on a French test whose results were sent to some national organization. I had remembered taking the test, but really didn't think that I had excelled in it. I later studied Greek in Bible College, and even covered about a fifth of a Teach-Yourself Hebrew book, but I never regarded myself as so proficient in any foreign language that I could operate in a country where that language was exclusively used. The best I can do, even now, is to recognize certain words and know how to look things up. I went to the teacher later in the day to find out about how it came about. She told me that all of the scores were so low that she had been embarrassed to send one in, but because mine was the highest, she sent mine in, and I won the honor for our school. So, now you know why I, for one, am so highly honored.

When God gives honors, they are real honors. They are based on even lower scores than my French score (the teacher didn't tell me what the percentage number was). In fact, they're based on a zero points F-minus grade. It was so bad that we weren't just put on suspension. We were denied the possibility of graduation ever on the bases of our grades. God, however, didn't take our grades when He honored us. He took Jesus' grades and applied them to our transcripts and that made all the difference in the world.

God didn't do all this so that His people could get a swelled head. He did it that they might be holy.

No one likes to be just the same as everyone else, but there is a fine line in which we aren't to stand out too much and enter the status of being weird. We like to blend in to a certain extent and be one of the gang and yet be serious to it all at the same time.

Distinctions are what always set people apart. Whether it's the stars on the Sneetches (or lack of them) or the animals that are more equal than others, they are seen in their differences as being better or worse than others. What God is doing for us is not a mere superficial cosmetic difference, but a genuine difference. That is one of the meanings of the word, holy. It is to be different and not set apart for common use. In other words, in God's hutch we're the fine china reserved for state dinners.

Being a holy people is being a people like God. It is being out of step with the world, but in step with Him. that's why it says to be holy unto Him. We're not just different for Him, but different unto Him. That's part of being a living sacrifice. We are to rise to God and not fall to the level of the world around us. We do this because He, Yahweh, is our God. We're beholden to Him alone and to no other.

The only way ultimately to blend in and stand out all at the same time is to love. That's the thing that can only be done without an ulterior motive, without in some way trying to control or herd someone else by loving them into doing it your way.

When we do this, we're not just doing something grand that might ring to our credit as in "Oh, what a good church are we!" This is simply living up to what God has intended us to be all along. Sometimes that doesn't amount to much, but in this case it amounts to everything. God has intended that we would be a premier example of what His grace and power can do with people.

Exodus 6:7
23 January 2021

Then. After and as a result of or leading to. This is a word that takes us from one place to another.

They are in bondage at the present moment. Verse 6 describes the releases. God is prophesying as to what He will do with them.

Before, God was a god of three families - Abraham, Isaac, Jacob. Now, He will be a God of a whole covenant nation. God always moves bigger, never smaller.

I will take you. This is more than the farmer takes a wife. He could take any wife, almost, who would have him, but God is more particular than that. He takes a people whom He is going to shape and grow. He takes them, not because they are great to begin with, but because of His knowledge of what He can do with or through them. They still have to be willing. In Dickens' David Copperfield, a fellow carved the words "Barkis is willing" on his cart. He didn't know how to express himself, so he made the carving and asked David Copperfield to pass the message on to the lady he was willing to mellow.

God knows how to express himself. He is willing to do more than enter into a social relationship with us. He is willing to save us. We, though, like the wives in both illustrations, have to be willing. We can only do it, though, after the fact of the call to come to God.

I will take you. This is not merely to prefer you, but actually to take you for His own people. in the ancient world, they thought of their deities as connected with either people groups or places. Our God is connected with us as His people and heaven as His place.

My people. They become, in this way, not merely His possession or chattel, but His responsibility.

A baby is more than a cute fun person. He requires care and nurture. You can't just leave him to himself. God gives us what we need in the same way, and even more than that, he grows us in a way that no human parent can grow a child by giving us the Holy Spirit to be inside us.

We bear the mark on our forehead, as it says in the book of Revelation, as a warning to the devil that he is not to mess with us. He tries, anyway, but God won't let him do anything in the end.

We are God's people. that was true of the Old Testament covenant people. it's true of the New Testament covenant people. we are grafted in alongside one another. It's not that we are attached to the Jews, but that Jew and Gentile are attached alike to the tree, that is to God Himself.

When God takes us He doesn't forget us. We are engraved on

the palms of His hands as Isaiah 49:16 puts it. He never minimizes us or ignores us. he maximizes us and pays attention to us. We are not Willie Lomans to Him, Willie Loman being a character from the play, "The Death Of A Salesman" of whom his wife said that he was basically dying of no respect.

Attention must be paid to every person. If you don't let God pay attention to you, someone else will, and it won't be to your good. it will be like Fagan and the boys who picked pockets for him in another Dickens work, Oliver Twist.

I will be your God. there's no doubt about that. The doubt is about us. Will we make God our God. The great example of that is Yahweh vs Baal on Mt. Carmel. At the end of that contest, the people shouted, "Yahweh, He is God." Who in their right mind would want Ball as their god after that, but people did. Guess they weren't in their right minds.

We want the God who can and will send fire, send manna, part the sea and the river, conquer the entrenched kingdoms of Canaan, send His son, send Him again, and who is listening to what Jesus is saying about us in the interval between the two sendings of Him. My Name Is Known. I wrote a song by that title, not because I'm so clever at lyrics, but because it is true.

God is big enough to encompass the universe and us and all that concerns us. He claims us. Baal, to name just one, never claimed anyone. They had to claim him, as it were. It was the same with Astarte or Moloch or any other so-called "god".

The first two things here about what God dd. Now, the question is, what will they do? I assume that if they don't do this, they will lose out. .

God is calling them to an assessment of faith, not merely to a fact which is known. did anyone see God bring them out? no. They saw what God did. Some of these things might have happened on their own some time or another, but not all ten of them to the degree they did.

Disease is not discriminating, only affecting the first born and not the siblings. Some diseases have been more prevalent among certain groups, but not pinpointed like that.

We know that He is Yahweh, our Elohim. That's the first part. Do you know Him? That's a powerful question. I recently heard part of a recording of a message by S. M. Lockridge which asked and answered that question. We are to know Him. no mask will keep us from knowing Him.

He is the Lord your God. This is existence speaking. He brought you act. That is action in the real world in real time in actual

186

experience. God didn't just plague the bad guys. He rescued His own. He brought them out. There was release from under the bondage. They were not going to be bound again. They were free.

We're never totally "free" of all restraint. We have laws governing our homes and activities and jobs and vehicles. No one gets to do whatever they want to do. These were free to do as they wished within the borders of the law. That was a broad border compared to the bondage of the Egyptians.

God says He brought them out, even though it hadn't happened yet. When God says it, it's **that** sure.

We are God's people. He is our God. we have been brought out of sin. It's all about relationship and reality.

Exodus 25:20
30 January 2021

Let's diagram this thing out as to what it is and what it means. I've heard about the mercy seat and the cherubim all my life. I can remember making a tabernacle model out of paper in Vacation Bible School. I've been to the Tabernacle presentation at the Mennonite Interpretive Center in Lancaster, Pennsylvania. But, I don't think I've ever thought this through like am going to do now.

1.   Cherubim With Wings Spread Upward

These are spiritual beings. In Psalm 18:10, God rode on the back of one of them. We're not talking naked babies here.

Their main feature seems to be the wings. The wings are spread upward, not straight out as in the depiction in "Raiders Of The Lost Ark". It could be that they are either all the way up or turned so that the inside of the wing points upward. I can see points made by either one of those possibilities.

Usually, the underside is turned to the ground in flight. If turning them up while holding them flat out is what it means here, they are affirming that their support comes from heaven and not from nature.

In application to us, our orientation is to be upward and supernatural. We can talk about this world all we want, but unless we're looking above, we're not looking the right place. Our posture should show that we are not in harmony with this world.

If these wings are all the way up, then the wings are so positioned to push toward heaven. wings in themselves imply unrestricted mobility with regard to all directions in the air. Birds don't always do that in a smart way. I had one almost fly into my car on the way to the journaling group the day I wrote the initial entry. Maybe he knew what he was doing, skimming so close to death, but he startled me.

These are not in the business of startling anyone, but of taking man's deficiencies to God for healing. Spiritual means are always open to us and requested of us. in this case, it was the high priest in conjunction with the cherubim going this. Now, it is our High Priest, Jesus, in conjunction with us Christians, of all people, doing it. we are a party to this. Our High Priest bypasses the cherubim and makes room for us in the equation.

2.   Covering The Mercy Seat With Their Wings

However the wings are positioned, they cover. This is not to obscure it, but protect it from all adverse elements and forces. The only thin that is to be there is the blood because this is all only of God, and that's all He would accept there.

These, while they are made of gold (verses 18), are a declaration that this is so.   No high priest could see this and think that atonement was **his** doing.

The mercy seat was atop the ark, but it more than just a fancy lid. It's the place where things happen. We're told of its existence and dimensions in verse 17. It's approximately 45 inches by 27 inches or 3 feet 9 inches by 2 feet 4 inches. This was a target, so to speak, that the blood couldn't miss.

The term mercy seat may not be the best or only translation of this as many commentators have pointed out, but we've got the idea. This is the place where God does something about what **we** have done. The mercy seat is covered to keep what takes place there in it's place, but the covering does not keep it from God. I don't think we can say that God doesn't see the sin anymore because of this. God sees and knows, but He forgives and gives mercy there.

There is an element of covering connected with holiness and godliness. It is not out there exposed to all things where it can be diluted or dirtied or disabled or disbelieved.

The wings are not, in this particular, for bearing them up, but for covering the mercy seat. The cherubim aren't going anywhere. They will not desert the place where we are freed from our sin.

3.   Facing One Another

Each sees what the other is, what he is doing, what is happening. This creates a unity which keeps the wings in place. They have a guard over one another.

We all know the value of watching, both positively and negatively. I never take that last cookie when someone is watching. People do what we inspect, not what we expect. I didn't make that last sentence up, just repeated it. I've seen a couple of attributions for it on the internet, but none seem to be conclusive since it seems to have been in print circulation before the fellow who it was attributed to put it out there, so I'll just use it without claming to have invented it.

Those are two worldly ideas, but I think the face to face is a mutual accountability for these are more than statues. They showed us on earth what the cherubim were probably doing in heaven. it doesn't say that, but I extrapolate it out from it.

When we are doing what God wants, we can look one another squarely in the face. From the next section it appears that the bodies are facing one another, but they're not looking at one another, but are each aware of what the other is looking at. They're both watching God at the same time. When we're looking at God, we don't have time to criticize or scrutinize anyone else.

4.   The Faces Are Toward The Mercy Seat

The point of the mercy seat, from the name of it, is not what the high priest does, but what God does.

Are we facing what God is doing? Are we expecting it to be done, then seeing it e done, then waiting for more to be done? Or, are we acting like Sally who said on the second day of school, "I went to kindergarten yesterday. Why do I have to go back?"

These are made of gold and always look. We're not just to be as good as gold, but better than gold.

At that time, we couldn't get where they were. Now, through Jesus, our confessed sins go to God direct. We are to look for mercy and expect it. Even the sinner can expect it AFTER he repents and comes into Jesus. (Of course, then he's no longer a sinner, but a Saint."

This was not just for them then. It is for us now.

* *

Index